GAMEPLAN
WORKBOOK

The Complete
Strategy Guide
to go from
Starter Kit to Silver

Sarah Harnisch
Young Living Diamond

Contents

THE GAMEPLAN COMPREHENSIVE STRATEGY WORKBOOK

HOW TO USE THIS BOOK

This workbook is written for both those both brand new to Young Living as well as those who have been working the business for a while. How can it be helpful for both? Let me explain.

To the brand new business builders...

This is a tool to help you see your business plan clearly and set tangible goals. It's for those of you who need to pour over the words in Gameplan and write them out to get them cemented in your minds. Walk the paths of hope with me throughout this workbook. Put it all on paper. Take a look inside your notes every six months and see how close you have gotten to attaining the rank of your dreams. It works! If you speak life over your dreams, it's amazing what starts to happen.

A woman once told me she didn't feel right praying for large things. She said that there were people starving all over the world, and it was immoral to pray for such a large income.

Hear my heart, weary mom, weary dad, and overworked worker: the desires of your heart are not yours. They were planted there by a much bigger God--One who has dreams for you that you can't even fathom. So chase the dreams. Put feet to your hopes. Dare to put them on paper, pray them aloud, and put one foot in front of another as you get closer and closer to the vision you see for your life, to the vision that was laid out over you before you were even born. You have permission to dream large. And you have permission to get there.

How can you help the widows, the poor and the sick when the head gasket is out in your car and you are short for your student loan payments this month? You can't pour into others when you are drowning. I believe with all my heart that the Lord wants abundance for His children. We just never claim it. We never believe it. And so it passes us by.

Never again. Your period of poverty is over. The famine has ended. And it's time to make some changes. It's time to have a Gameplan.

It's time to hit the goals you have thought about for years, but never actually ran toward. This is your book, dreamer. Let's lay out some plans together, side by side. I am the momma that had nothing—spent 36 years in poverty—and went from starter kit to Platinum in 17 months with no friend circle and no time. If I can do it, you can do it. It takes rolling up your sleeves, planning where you are going, and what you are moving toward. This book is your plan. You will be blown away at what the Lord does as you speak this aloud, and move.

The only thing holding you back from Royal Crown Diamond is you.

It's time to run.

Are you ready?

To the leaders...

You've read Gameplan and are ready to take your team to the next level by investing in your leaders. This workbook is the tool you need to effectively and consistently build into your team. You need to turn the dreams in your head into a moving, growing team. Gameplan is a compilation of many Oil Ability leaders' tried and true methods, all in one place. I found that there was great material out there, but you needed a stack of books to train your team. The Gameplan book and workbook compiles it in an easy to understand format and tailors it directly to your team. It's customized strategy.

Vicki Opfer is a Young Living Royal Crown Diamond that wrote a fantastic document called "Heart Centered Sharing." In it, she lays out numbers of what sharing looks like for her business. She says if you enroll 2 people a month, at the end of the year, you will have a team of 25 and your check will be about 100 dollars higher. But if you enroll 2 people a month and train them how to enroll their own 2 people, (and they in turn train those 2 people how to enroll just 2 people), at the end of the year you have 531,440 people in your organization and a Young Living check of over 10-thousand dollars a month.

It's all in the training.

My hope is that you will take this workbook and use it to train your own teams. We offer bulk pricing on the Gameplan book and workbook at oilabilityteam.com to make your training easy and affordable. If you were to take the Gameplan book and workbook and train just 2 of your top leaders, and then train them how to use it to train their leaders, your organization would grow exponentially.

What does training look like? There are 24 chapters in Gameplan and 24 chapters in the workbook. They were written side by side. Ask your leaders to read a chapter in Gameplan, do the workbook pages for that chapter, then meet and review them. Offer incentives for completing the chapters. Perhaps you do a 24-day bootcamp with your leaders online with both books. Or maybe you opt to take it slower and meet in person or online once a week over 24 weeks. The neat thing is there truly isn't a wrong way of training. Just tailor it to your team with a pace you can handle. By the end of this workbook, you'll have surefire methods of how to market and host classes, develop warm leads, do follow up, train your leaders, and more.

The ultimate goal is to get your leaders to see where this goes. If they write out their dreams and wishes and see that how they are spending their time at their 40-hour-a-week job is not going to get them there, it will not be hard to motivate them to commit 2 hours a week to hold a class. The 2 hours a week, over time, can build into a sustainable business through consistency and tenacity that will replace the 40 hours they are pursuing daily. Your task is to train them how to dream, and where to start.

Then train them how to train their own leaders.

That is the whole key to Gameplan. If you want to see the greatest results, don't keep these books tucked away on a shelf for your eyes only. Use them how they were meant to be used, to inspire and equip your leaders.

Then teach them to how to duplicate.

You have this, Diamond. Get out there and show them how it's done!

My name is

_____

And I am a Young Living Royal Crown Diamond.

CHAPTER 1

WHY LAUNCH A YOUNG LIVING BUSINESS

Recap 10 reasons why it's smart to launch a Young Living business. (Hint: Scour the "Why Launch a Young Living Business" chapter in the Gameplan book to find your answers! There are more than 10 reasons!)

1) _____

2) _____

3) _____

4) _____

5) _____

6) _____

7) _____

8) _____

9) _____

10) _____

Which one is your favorite? Circle it.

Check out the Young Living income disclosure guide. Write down a few goals. Write down what that average income would do for your family, and what changes you could make.

I want to make _____ rank by _____ , 20____.

I will have an average income of $_____ a month.

When I attain that rank, I can:

Now vision cast with me. Did you check out the income disclosure guide? That's a tally of what all Young Living distributors everywhere are making. What would you do with a Royal Crown Diamond monthly income of $241,324 dollars?

Write down 3 things that would be on your ultimate bucket list.

1) _____

2) _____

3) _____

Do you believe that's attainable? Tell me the truth! Do you believe network marketing truly works? Do you believe that if you put the hard work in, and be tenacious, and be consistent—that you can get there?

YOUR ASSIGNMENT: WRITE YOUR WHY

Take a few moments and write out your "why". Why are you a Young Living distributor? Be real. When I first started, it truly was just to get the oils in my home. I could not afford them with 5 kids, one special needs son in a pricey school, 70-thousand dollars in student loans, and a mortgage. It then morphed into seeing the miracles around me every day from those oils working. And after about 6 months, my Young Living income surpassed my full time job. That's when I realized I truly had a passion for helping people do what John and I had just done. One year and one month after getting my starter kit, I retired from 18 years of waking up at 3 a.m. for my shift. Two years and two months after getting my starter kit, my husband also came home for good. I was 37 and he was 41. It is possible!

My why now is to raise as many Diamonds as possible. I believe you can truly do what you were called and created to do when you have the time economy and the financial freedom to pour into those around you, and aren't always depleted, operating in emergency mode. That's my why. After living in decades of extreme poverty, my why is to raise as many people out of it as possible. That's why this book isn't just for our team. It's for anyone who has a hope of getting out of their cycle of survival.

It's time for you to put your pencil to the paper. Tell me your why; your hopes and your dreams. Some of mine are:

-to get a little boat and take my kids out on the Fingerlakes of New York where we live. My grandparents had a sailboat when I was growing up, and I went on to get scuba certified at 14 years old and fall in love with the water. I have always wanted my kids to experience some of my memories.

-to take a vacation once a year with all 5 of our kids, and to go away on a weekend every other month alone with my husband that is at least 2 nights long

-to travel and take my homeschoolers with me to explore and see the world

-to pay off every penny of debt we've accrued, our home too, so we can live on 10 percent and tithe 90 percent of our income to ministries that tug on our hearts

-to mentor young couples and single moms so they can have financial freedom

-to visit our family all over the country—and stay longer than a few days

-to rest. To take a week at a time and just read in my hammock and weed my garden and go on long walks in the woods and sleep late and take a nap.

That's my bucket list.

Now tell me your yours. Tell me why you're doing this business. Tell me your dreams. What do you want out of this journey? Be brave. And be real. And truly think it through. Then as you do each of these things, cross them off and write the date that it happened right beside it.

MY WHY

BONUS ASSIGNMENT

If you are still in doubt about network marketing being a wise choice for you, I have an extra assignment for you. I want you to go to one of my favorite network marketer's sites, ericworre.com, and check out his store. His "Go Pro" book is one of my favorite network marketing books of all time, and worth a top-down read. But I have a different assignment for you: I want you to invest in the "Rise of the Entrepreneur" DVD. If you still truly believe your 9 to 5 job is the best way to care for your family, that will be the best 52 minutes you spend this year. It's loaded with statistics and facts about network marketing that will forever change the way you look at the 40-hour work week.

CHAPTER 2

SARAH'S STORY

If you read Gameplan Chapter Two, you have now read my dirt. Every family has dirt. Our family's dirt was alcoholism, drug addiction, mental health, and poverty. I believe that the cycle can be broken. I believe` you can change the course of your family's path, by first believing it's possible, then coming up with a plan on how to get from point A to point B, and taking small steps to get there.

YOUR ASSIGNMENT: WRITE YOUR STORY

Take some time and write out your story. Write down where you have been. In bullet points, share some of the hardest moments of your life. Then at the end, I want you to write in the largest letters possible: FAMINE OVER. I AM FREE.

CHAPTER 3

HOW TO BEGIN: A QUICK-START TRAINING GUIDE WITH JUST 2 TIPS

Can it really be that simple? Grab a simple 101 Script, get a few people in front of you and read it? Then rinse and repeat?

I tell you from the deepest places of my heart, there is no magic pill to the rank John and I hit. It was just raw work. It was rolling up my sleeves and getting out there and doing it. You don't need to hit the pavement as hard as I did, but if you commit to 4-6 classes a month (that's about an 8 hour a month time commitment), that's what it's taken for the Silvers on the Oil Ability team to go Silver in Six. We have 11 Silvers on the team at the moment with another 8 set to hit it in the next 4-8 weeks, and every single one of them did it in 6 months, simply by holding 4 classes a month and doing good follow up. Then when someone sold a kit, they immediately trained them using the Teacher Training script in the back of Gameplan.

Is it worth it? Is an extra $2,000 to $3,000 a month worth doing this business alongside your life for a season, until you can drop a few things off your plate? The strategy has been the same from each of the Diamonds I have interviewed. Every time I ask them what the key to their success was, I get the same answer: classes. Class after class after class. There is no chincy way of ranking. You just have to get out there and do it.

YOUR ASSIGNMENT: PREPARE FOR YOUR FIRST CLASS

Photocopy the 101 Script out of the back of the Gameplan book and begin practicing it. It takes about 20 minutes to read it aloud if it's just you and a mirror. If you're doing it in front of someone, it takes about 30 minutes. Read it through 10 times, over 1-2 weeks. On time 10, that's it. You're out of practice. Then it's time to do it in front of someone. (Or several someones).

Place a check mark in a box each time you read through the script to yourself.

☐ ☐ ☐ ☐ ☐ ☐ ☐ ☐ ☐ ☐

Now I want you to pick your mom or best friend, someone who won't laugh if you lose your place, and have at it.

When you make it through your first live audience, get out there and schedule a class. Read it in your living room. Read it at a restaurant with three people over a piece of cheesecake. Once you get over the fear of that first class, and your unknowns are no longer unknown, it's time to take this seriously.

Go to the store and buy a planner. You can buy one at the Dollar Store if you're on a tight budget, or you can order the ibloom planner that I use and love so much (ibloom.co). Commit to going all in. Locate four free locations you can use in the next month. (They can be your living room if you like. That's where my first classes were!) Book them. Set up Facebook events for them. Have 3 different friends invite 50 friends to each of those events. And get out there and start putting some movement to your dreams.

Got all that? Here's review of your homework for this chapter so far:

☐ Practice the 101 lecture 10 times

☐ Practice it in front of someone you know well who can give you pointers

Now you're ready to actually start! Get your first 4 classes up on Facebook, market them, and have people start inviting. It's go time. If you need wording on how to market your class, take a peek in the Gameplan book.

BONUS ASSIGNMENT: CREATE A VISION BOARD

Prepping for your first class is not the only assignment for this chapter. I also want you to have some tangible dreams you can see every single day, so it keeps you going. Here is your mission: go to a craft store, spend $3 on a canvas board, and spend an afternoon cutting up some magazines. Cut out pictures of your dreams (for me it would be that boat!) Cut out words that you want spoken over your business. Print the rank you want to be off the Young Living website. Pull a check out of your checkbook, write the number you want to see on it for your monthly pay, and sign it with Mary Young's name—and glue that thing with tons of glue on that vision board. Put it where you constantly see it. As you pass it, read the words on the board aloud. Speak life over your dreams. Then, when you are chicken about booking a class, look back at the board and remember why you're doing this. It's because Young Living is a way out. But you have to put the work in and start digging.

Here's a photo of my vision board. I know it sounds chincy to sit there with paper and scissors—you're a grown adult, right? But I'll tell you, there is something magical that happens when you put your dreams to paper. They start to come true. Maybe part of it is that you can see where you are going and you have an end game. Part of it is that you are speaking like this every single day, and there is power in the spoken word. (God created the world with the spoken word—it worked for Him!) You're seeing your goals every single day—and there is power in visualizing where you are heading. Either way, it works. Only six months after making this thing, more than half of it has already happened. Put tangible items on the board, things you know you can do in a year or less. Then move toward the goal.

CHAPTER 4

AVOIDING PITFALLS: THE 6 MISTAKES EVERY STAGNANT BUSINESS BUILDER MAKES

List the 6 mistakes I detail in Chapter 4:

1) ....

2) ....

3) ....

4) ....

5) ....

6) ....

Which one do you think is your biggest pitfall?

1) ....

Why? ....

....

....

....

....

YOUR ASSIGNMENT: FOCUS ON THE SOLUTION

Write up a plan (or several!) for avoiding or overcoming you biggest pitfall. What is the solution to avoiding that mistake? Show me what it looks like for you to learn from my mistakes and avoid these pitfalls. Use phrases like "I will..." and "I won't..."

CHAPTER 5

OVERCOMING EXCUSES AND FINDING YOUR NICHE

I was sneaky in this chapter. I titled it "finding your niche". But truly, it's a chapter that blasts you from the start about defying excuses. Why is identifying them so important? Because it can emotionally cripple your business if you believe lies. I wrote down some of the top excuses I hear in Young Living. In fact, I listed 11 different excuses in the opening to the chapter. Can you identify some of them again, with the response to each excuse?

_____

_____

_____

_____

_____

I am sure you've heard all those excuses before. But tell me which one you think describes you the most:

_____

_____

_____

_____

_____

YOUR ASSIGNMENT: MOVE BEYOND YOUR EXCUSES

Now I want you to write down you way out of it. What is the opposite of that statement above? How can you fight your own negativity in your head? Walk me through it by writing it down. If you cannot think of a way out of that thought pattern, simply write down the opposite.

Example: "I don't know anyone." Opposite: "I do have a friend circle of _____ people, and it is growing every day. I will be successful at this, because I am a Young Living Diamond. A Diamond does not make excuses. They cut through mountains. I am finding a way around my mountain without a word of complaint, because I know where my hard work will lead me. And it's worth the fight."

Now to the second part of the chapter. There are many ways of sharing Young Living. While I still believe with all my heart that in-person classes with as many people as you can is the fastest way to grow, I know that's not possible for everyone in every season. Check by the options below that you believe you may be good at.

- ☐ mailing out DVD's or audio CD's from oilabilityteam.com and doing good follow up
- ☐ having an eye for talent and raising business builders
- ☐ putting oils on people. Handing out samples and doing good follow up
- ☐ meeting people one on one over your lunch break or for dinner and going over the 101 lecture
- ☐ putting up flyers at local businesses and connecting with the owners to hold classes at chiropractic offices, natural food stores, bulk food stores, Yoga studios, and more

- writing, blogging, and vlogging online. Doing online Facebook live or zoom or blab classes. Marketing heavily before and doing great follow up after

- hand written notes, flyers and samples. You're a gifted letter writer

- an eye for sales. Learning to work paid leads and prospects and branching out to new people you've never met

- tithing and praying and letting the Lord grow your business organically, but acting deliberately on every single person He puts in your path

You may have circled one or two. I'll tell you straight up I've used every single one of these methods. And they all work. In-person classes work the fastest. But if you need a place to start, and you see another gifting in yourself, go for it. Use one of the other methods above. The key is being consistent, working your business as a business, and doing knockout follow up.

If people sense that you are real and they are not being hunted solely for a starter kit, and you can pass along your passion, you will grow.

My advice is to diversify. In the span of a month, do three in-person classes, give it a shot at an online class, and get oils on people. Get into a vendor event and meet some new faces. Use all the methods. But make sure they all have a component of the 101 Script in them, or you won't get results.

Let me flesh that out for you for a bit. If you do a specialty class like a beauty school, incorporate some of the 101 notes while they are doing their facials and have the masque on, and make sure you tell them where to get the starter kit. If you are doing a make-and-take class, make them watch a 10-minute version of the 101 class on a DVD before you start—maybe something you shoot ahead of time. If you are doing a vendor event, hand out 101 audio CD's to every person that fills out a form to win a gift basket. (They cost about a dollar each). If you give someone an oil at work to help them out, practice the "if I, would you" mentality (see Chapter 12 of Gameplan for this strategy) and ask them if you give them the oil for free, wwould they listen to the audio 101 CD on the way home from work in the car? Always make sure there's a response from the person you are working with—or your work is for naught.

Can I throw in one more thing? It's a principle that I think is very important, because I get requests weekly for people wanting to jump ship with the team they are on and move to the Oil Ability team. It drives me crazy. If you are not successful where you are, you won't be successful on our team. How do I know? Success depends on you. It has nothing to do with your upline, how much you know, how kind the people are around you, how much support you have, or how many resources you are given. Blaming your upline is another excuse.

BONUS ASSIGNMENT

There is a wonderful quote in Eric Worre's "Go Pro" book that I love. (It's a fantastic book that will help you with the emotional side of network marketing—pick it up at ericworre.com and give it a good read.) I'd like you not just to read this paragraph, but to write it on a 3x5 card and put it on your bathroom mirror, and repeat it to yourself when you see it. You have no one to blame for your failure but you.

From page 103 of his book:

"If I succeed in this business, it's going to be me that creates the success, not my upline. And if I fail in this business, it's going to be me that creates the failure, not my team or my upline. I am the difference between success and failure. My upline is here to guide me, but they cannot do the work for me. They are here to work with me, but not for me."

CHAPTER 6

YOUR GREATEST TOOL: A DETAILED TOUR OF THE YOUNG LIVING VIRTUAL OFFICE

For this one, you'll have to go tech savy on me. Before you go any further in this book, find your username and password (the one you wrote down when you bought your starter kit.) If you can't find it, call Young Living directly and they'll issue you a new password—it's super easy.

Once you have that, go to youngliving.com and click "sign in." Then you'll be at the screen where you'll need that username and password. Every single person that gets a starter kit, whether they are selling or not, should have been trained by their upline to log in and check out their virtual office. At the very least, they have to know how to order more product. My advice is to scope out 2 buttons first. At the top in the center is the "Getting Started" tab. It's loaded with 3 and 4-minute videos that will really lay the groundwork for your understanding of Young Living. It's important that you spend some time on Young Living's Seed to Seal site (one of the links on the Getting Started page). It is what sets us apart from every other oils company in the world.

If you want to kick it up a notch, and really want to understand why Young Living is a pioneer, go to "Quick Order" and type in "D. Gary Young: The World Leader In Essential Oils". A book with a purple cover will pop up with a photo of Gary on it. If you read that book, it will put to rest any question in your mind about the stewardship and integrity of Young Living, and what it took to become a billion dollar oils company. My eyes still well up when I look at what Gary went through to bring us the purest oils in the world. It was such an incredible journey. For those of you that think Gameplan has sucked all the brain cells out of your brain, don't dismay. This book is mostly pictures. It's a picture journey of Young Living's story.

Back to the Virtual Office. After you've watched all the videos in the "Getting Started" tab, it's time to do some reading online. The next tab I want you to check out is "Member Resources." That one is loaded with documents to read. Hone in on "Policies and Procedures" and devour it. Those are all the rules of Young Living. For example, did you know that you can't sign your spouse and get two Young Living checks in your home, unless they were already a distributor before you were married? It's good to know those rules. Print them off, put them in a binder, read them once, and move on.

When you have a lazy afternoon, just click through all the other tabs under Member Resources. Get familiar with the powerpoint presentations, Young Living University, and all the shareable graphics and FDA compliance information. There is SO much on that tab.

Once you're done with those 2 buttons, grab Gameplan and follow along. Click on the buttons across the top of your dashboard and the buttons to the left, following the graphics in the book, and become familiar with where everything is.

Got all that? Let me lay it out again:

YOUR ASSIGNMENT: GET FAMILIAR WITH THE VIRTUAL OFFICE

☐ Click on the "Getting Started" tab and watch all the videos

☐ Order the "D. Gary Young: The World Leader In Essential Oils" book off the Quick Order button and read it (it's worth it!)

☐ Click on "Member Resources" and lose yourself in all the resources they have pooled together for us

☐ Open your Gameplan book and go to Chapter 6 and the Virtual Office tour, and click through each of the buttons across the top and left side of the virtual office, getting familiar with where things are.

Make sure you understand the Rank Qualification button. I'm on that myself a couple of times a day. It's your end game. It's your goal post. It's where you're heading. You're never going to get where you're going if you don't know what the end game is. Set a goal, perhaps a small one at first, and chart it under that button.

For those of you that picked up this workbook, I am going to give you a little bonus section not in the Gameplan book as a thank you. Because you are going through the "Rank Qualification button", I want to talk you through early in the workbook on exactly how to rank up.

BONUS TRAINING: RANKING STRATEGIES

In this section I'm going to go a little deeper into the ranking strategies I laid out in Gameplan. If you are a details person and really want more examples of what it looks like to apply a winning strategy to building your business, this bonus training is just for you.

I know it's easy to see Star rank and set your sites on that, with little beyond. But those first two ranks (Star and Senior Star) are just there to get your attention. They're there to show you that you can do this—to give you vision. The first true goal you need to have in mind is to hit Executive, even from the very beginning. There is a reason for this. The whole foundation of the start of your business stems from that. From the moment you make a decision to be a Young Living distributor, put your sights on Executive so you have your chess pieces in the right places to rank even higher. According to the "rank qualification" tab, you need a PGV of 1000, an overall OGV of 4000, and 2 legs with 1000 OGV in each.

Before I give you more strategy, do the homework assignment below so you know what I'm talking about.

Tell me what a few terms mean so you can learn Young Living-ease. (If you need a hint, there is a Young Living-ease glossary in Appendix M of Gameplan to help you out.)

OGV: ....

PGV: ....

Upline: ....

Downline: ....

Legs: ....

Essential Rewards: ....

Why do you want to be on ER? (This is one of the key secrets to ranking up!)

_____

_____

What it takes to attain the rank of silver: (OGV, PGV, legs):

_____

_____

Back to strategy.

From the first moment of your business, I want you to be looking for two leaders. For the first month or two, depending on how many classes you hold each month, just sign everyone under you. You are the sponsor and you are the enroller. You are waiting to see who "pops"—who turns around and sells a kit to someone else. That may be your first leader. Get them trained—stat—while they are on fire—with the Teacher Training in the Appendix of the Gameplan book. Then gift the Gameplan book to them after their first class as a reward, so they can start their oily business on the right foot.

If no one "pops" after your first 8 classes or so, I want you to continue signing people under you directly until 1 of 2 things happens: you reach 1000PGV (that's volume outside your 2 legs), or you pick up another business builder that's willing to let you host classes for them and is spending the 100pv a month to get a paycheck.

Why do you need loose people (non-business builders) under you? What exactly is PGV? It's your Personal Group Volume—the sales that come from people on your team who aren't in a qualifying leg. It's five or six people under you on Essential Rewards, ordering each month. They have no one under them. They are just loose members on your team.

Once you have 1000 PGV established, every single kit sale from that point on goes under one of two people who are going to be your legs. Your first goal is Executive: that's 4000 OGV volume, and 10 kits on each of those two legs. Ideally, those two leaders are working in tandem with you and you're leaning on their friend circles to pull off classes.

The benefit to building this way is:

1) Your PGV will be established and you'll never have to worry about it again, all the way to Royal Crown Diamond. You must have 1000 PGV at all times or you lose your check once you hit Silver. You will have laid the groundwork.

2) You'll have two leaders to build under, the same two that you need to hit the next rank of Silver.

How do you know who to place where? I just go back and forth between the two legs, and keep them at about the same volume. If one of your legs is at 400 OGV and the other is at 800 OGV, I'd be teaching under the 400 OGV rank because you need it at 1000 OGV to rank.

So here are the steps again, in layman's terms:

For your first 2 months or 8 classes, sign everyone under you as both sponsor and enroller. The goal is to build up 1000 PGV, $1000 in sales outside your two legs.

During this time, watch to see who "pops". If someone pops right away, and you're teaching four classes a month, teach one or two classes for them, and the other two classes would go for your PGV—so they would go directly under you.

If you teach for two months and have no leaders, have a good conversation with the people you have gotten on Essential Rewards that are excited about the oils. If they don't want a business, ask if they are willing to allow you to teach and build legs under them—so they can get their oils for free. If their answer is yes, then start using them as sponsor and you as enroller. Their requirement would be to spend 100 PV a month to get paid, and to open their friend circle to you. The payoff is free oils!

Once your PGV is established, all your attention goes on those two leaders. Every person goes under one of those two legs, and nowhere else, to help you get to Executive. From day one, your eye is on that rank, so you have your foundation laid for Silver and your PGV is in place.

One more tip: from the beginning, plug the business! I have never had a hard time finding business builders, because from my first class I was telling people why Young Living was the best job I'd ever had. Even if you just drop two or three lines in your 101 class, it will spark interest. Another way to raise business builders is to chase every 101 class with the 10 minute "Why Do Young Living as a Business" DVD on our website, oilabilityteam.com. It's amazing who moves on what they see—it's rarely the person I pick out of the crowd!

You have survived your only techie tour in this workbook! Congratulations! The rest of the book is much less strenuous on your brain!

CHAPTER 7

YOUNG LIVING MARKETING 101: HOW TO SHARE THE OILS

What is the truth about network marketing? Share it with me below.

Now, I want you to go to Youtube and watch a Pat Petrini video called "I Still Think It's A Pyramid Scheme." It's 3 minutes of your life that you'll never get back. But you'll love me for it. No one will ever be able to tell you that network marketing is a pyramid scheme again. You can find it by typing "I think it's a pyramid scheme" into the search engine on Youtube. After a few giggles, tell me what you learned.

I'm going to have you do a few outline exercises, because it's good for your soul. Finish these thoughts right out of the Gameplan book:

Never once have I

There are two things you need

You don't need to become

The trick isn't

Great job! Now that you know Network Marketing is the real deal, I want you to walk me through the 8 steps to set up a Facebook event. It's time to get your first class on the road. You can't get off the ground if you don't teach.

1) ....

....

2) ....

....

3) ....

....

4) ....

....

5) ....

....

6) ....

....

7) ....

....

8) ....

....

YOUR ASSIGNMENT: PRACTICE MARKETING AN EVENT

Now go to Facebook and try setting up your own event. Don't spend a lot of time getting the wording just right—we're gonna work on that in the next chapter. For now just practice uploading a banner and getting a few lines in the description box. Don't worry, no one will see your practice event unless you take the final step of inviting people! This is just so that you learn how to do this, and see how easy it is! When you have a description handy and a photo selected for the banner, it only takes about two minutes to set up an event.

Now tell me, what are the 4 steps to simple marketing?

1) _____

2) _____

3) _____

4) _____

What are the 9 steps to holding an online class?

1) _____

2) _____

3) _____

4) _____

5) _____

6) _____

7) _____

8) _____

9) _____

BONUS ASSIGNMENT: FILM AN ONLINE CLASS INTRO

For the bold leaders out there: grab your cell phone, grab the first paragraph of the 101 Script, find a well-lit place without an echo, and try recording it. Just do a dry run. See what you look like on camera. Critique yourself. You can do this! Make sure the video is no longer then 3-4 minutes.

You now you see that you have everything it takes to shoot an entire 101 and upload it online. You can do this!

What about vendor events?

Go into them with the expectation of getting leads for classes, not selling oodles of starter kits. Write down 2 tips that you picked up from this section:

1) _____

_____

2) _____

_____

Talking to Cold Contacts

What did you think about the role playing exercise to gain business builders? I have had so many conversations just like that! The last 3 business builders I signed this week I met in random places: in airports, in restaurants, at the post office. It just takes a heart to see that people are dissatisfied.

- Try reading it through again imagining you're pitching it to someone you truly love, that you want to see set free from financial bondage.
- Practice the role play a few times so it's in your head when you come across someone who will be playing the other end live.

YOUR ASSIGNMENT: MAKE A LIST

This next assignment is going to take you a while. In fact, for people who like to walk away from a workbook and have it completely finished, this assignment is really going to irk you- because it's never quite done.

Today, I want you to start compiling a list of your warm market. In network marketing terms, these are people that know you—perhaps very well, like a family member, or just as an acquaintance. If they hear your name and they know who you are, they are your warm market.

For the first week, I want you to be really deliberate about putting this list together. After that, I want you to keep your workbook in a place where you have access to it regularly, and every time you come across someone you forgot, add their name to the list. After a month or so, leave your workbook at home and just text names to yourself of people that need to be on this list.

I set aside 5 pages of lines for you to write names, though you may end up needing far more. These are the people that you'll use to invite 50 people to your class events set up on Facebook, or when you have plateaued, to do one-on-one classes with.

Let me give you some ideas of where to draw from. Take the next few pages and make a list of every single person you know that should be introduced to oils. (That was a trick question. EVERY person you know should be introduced to oils.)

Start with Facebook. Go through your entire friend's list and add most of the names. Then go through your other social media outlets: Instagram, Pinterest, Twitter, your email account, LinkedIn, Snapchat, and any other place you may be connecting with people online.

After that, I usually comb through my address book—the one I use when I mail Christmas cards. Look through you cell phone for contacts you may have forgotten and add them. Think through the people you see at church, in small group, in your homeschool group or any activity for your kids at public school, in boy scouts, ballet, soccer, basketball, football, band, art club, or cheerleading.

Think about the paths you cross at the post office, and the woman that has sent your packages 40 times that knows your face. Think about your co-workers. Think about the neighbors on your street. Then think of your friends, and the friends they have had to their homes while you have been there. Think of all the people you run into doing the things that you love: running, reading, volunteering—any place your feet may go. Think of all your ties in the community: the chamber of commerce, the 5k that you ran, the car wash you took part in. Think about all your acquaintances that you see in passing, your spouse's coworkers and the friend that is always at your friend's home when you go over there.

Literally make a working list of every human you know. And put them on these next few sheets. When you are frustrated and can't fill classes, this is the place I want you to return to for inspiration. There are always people that have been missed for starter kits. One of the worst feelings in the world is seeing an old friend sign with someone they don't even know—because you never made contact with them. This is how to stop that from happening.

Why you need a list

Let me tell you a story. After I ranked Platinum, I got stuck there for 5 months. My OGV hovered between 120,000 and 150,000 every month. So I decided to take my own advice and take another look at my warm market (the people that I knew personally). What I discovered was that in my rush to diamond, I had totally left out some of my closest friends. Because I have a business Facebook page and do most of my oils posts there, there were people in my own family- close cousins, aunts, best friends—that had never been introduced to oils.

When you have a product that you deeply believe in, don't you want your family and friends to have it first? In my haste, I had forgotten the people I most loved. I had taught 182 classes in New York and Pennsylvania and completely left out the town I grew up in, the place I lived for 30 years: Chicago. So one morning, I sat down and made a list of my Chicago contacts only. 450 people. If I sold a kit to those people alone, I would have half the volume to get to diamond without another leader selling single kit. And my closest friends would be on my oils team.

Do not forget those closest to you. The worst thing that can happen is that they sign on another oils team because you never spoke up. It would hurt to have your best friend somewhere else! So be bold. Speak out. Have no fear.

And make your list. Right now. When you are done, contact 5 of those people every week. Start with a relationship. Listen to where they are. Form them to get to know their needs. And meet them where they are on their road.

Once you have thought of every person you know, carry this book with you for a while and keep adding names as you think of new places and faces. Then pick it up every few weeks and add to it. The list will be much longer then you thought it would.

One. Two. Three... GO.

You don't need to be an expert

There is just one more thing I want to throw in at the end of Chapter 7, because it's a roadblock to so many distributors. We hit it right at the end of the chapter. You don't need to be an expert to do network marketing.

For most of my life, people have relied on me as a news anchor to provide them with trustworthy, accurate information. In fact—they even rely on me to provide information that I have no idea about, like the weather forecast (never once have I been to a school for meteorology!) But here's the secret to being a news anchor: you just have to get really good at finding stuff. When I come into a newsroom, I first read about 39 newspapers online (I am speed reading folks, I am not THAT good), and I read 6 papers that are delivered to the door. Then I watch the networks—all 7 of them. By the time I go on, I know where the best soundbites are, the best facts, and the strongest writing. I have seen it all by 6 a.m. and I can see my entire shift in my head. I know what angle I will take my newscasts from.

That's sort of the way a Young Living business works. You don't need to download 100 years of aromatherapy and be an M.D. to make it work. Actually, even if you went for those credentials, you'd still not be able to share in the way that you want to, because once you are a distributor, you are an extension of Young Living Corporate, and you fall under all of the rules and regulations that the staff fall under because of the FDA. You are not allowed to use the oils to treat diseases. Titles mean nothing. Believe me though, it's a much better title to have distributor after your name, and know where that goes, then to go for a certification that won't bring the pay, relationships, time freedom, and growth you'll get from teaching classes and building a team. A distributorship is always the right way to go.

If your heart is to help people, the best thing you can do is get really good at understanding third party resources. Take a moment and list some of the top resources I've laid out for you below:

☐ ....

☐ ....

☐ ....

If there is one thing I want you to get out of this chapter, it's that you truly don't need to be an expert. You just need passion to share the oils. Compassion for where people are, without judgment. And tenacity to see it through to the end. Learn your tools and leave the expert advice to the experts. Then you'll rock Young Living.

CHAPTER 8

THE OIL ABILITY MARKETING SYSTEM: HOW TO FILL CLASSES WITHOUT KNOWING PEOPLE

Let's play a fill-in-the-blank game for this chapter, because so many of the concepts are terribly important for you to cut down on discouragement.

The trick to filling classes isn't who you know, it's _____

_____

The average person knows about _____

It's going to take a lot more than just you _____

_____

What is the Oil Ability Event Marketing System? Write it out.

1) _____

2) _____

3) _____

4) _____

5) _____

6) _____

Not convinced that you should be on Facebook? For 10 minutes, go to Youtube and type in "21st Century Social Media Trends." The information in that powerful video will astound you. And you'll want to get into social media. If your religious or moral beliefs prohibit it, don't sweat it. Young Living was successful as a company long before Facebook was ever created. Just keep doing in-person classes and great follow up, and you will get where you want to go.

Now let's work on writing. If you're a pretty rotten writer, don't sweat it. Gameplan has just saved you. Go ahead and steal my scripts and marketing. (You're not actually stealing it—you paid for it, silly. If you resell it, I will hunt you down, though.)

YOUR ASSIGNMENT: MARKET YOUR FIRST CLASS

If you think you do a pretty good job at getting your thoughts on paper, then you'll enjoy this homework assignment.

Take some time to write a (short) knockout paragraph to convince people to come to your 101 class. The good news is that you really only need to write it once, because you're always inviting 3 different people to invite 50 people to your classes. Your invitees should always be different, so there's no need to re-invent the wheel, unless you're teaching a different class outside the 101. (And I don't recommend that if you're just starting your business. Once you get people on Essential Rewards, I'll teach one specialty class to keep them interested and give them ideas. But my other 3 classes a month are always prospecting—always looking for new people on my team. The ratio is 3 101's to 1 specialty class, like Oils of the Bible or .)

Back to writing. (You thought you got out of it, didn't you??)

Give me a paragraph that will get someone who has never heard of essential oils into a seat in your class. Be enthusiastic and confident!

Now your task is to actually put this entire chapter into play. Get online, use that paragraph you wrote, set up an event and get 3 people to invite 50 people to it. Go on. Try it.

It's important that you don't just create an event and ask people to share it to their page. There is good marketing and there is bad marketing. Sharing an event is bad marketing—because people won't see any of your posts in the event unless they have actually been invited. It's the same thing if you're running a business page. I see people all the time put a ton of work into posting all day long, and they have 17 people on their page. Dude—if you only have 18 people on your business page, you should be plugging that page constantly (sharing a link to your business page) on your personal page, to garner interest.

☐ Put a check on that box once you've set up your first event. If you have the writing already done (which you do, because you did it above), you can get this sucker up in 10 minutes flat.

Do you need an image for the banner? Hop on over to Oil Ability with Sarah on Facebook, like my page (did you pick up on my marketing there? That was a savvy slip!) Then you have access to all my photos. Click on "photos" and take whatever you like—banner images, etc.... All of it is compliant.

Once that event is up, post in it once or twice a day using the photos from my Facebook page, or any other compliant source you have, like the Young Living blog (which is FANTASTIC.)

You should have 4-6 of these event set up every single month. I market them at the same time every day, first thing in the morning. You can even schedule your posts, so you don't have to be online at 12 noon to pop something up.

What If I Still Can't Fill Classes?

- ☐ listen to your warm market
- ☐ host classes in a public place
- ☐ be willing to travel
- ☐ teach online classes
- ☐ get more personal with your follow up and your invitations to class—have face-to-face interaction
- ☐ incorporate vendor events

Have you tried all the methods of filling classes? If you are stuck, try one of the methods above and see if it gets you moving again. From time to time, I tweak what I'm doing depending on what's going on in my life at the time, and if I feel my business has stalled. Always stay open to all options.

What did you think about the conversations in Chapter 8? The ones that give you an idea of how to invite someone—in 30 seconds flat—to your class? Or to catch a business builder's attention?

Return to those conversations and read them again in the Gameplan book, especially if you struggle with face-to-face interaction, or feel like you are forcing someone to make a decision.

☐ Go read them through three times today.

Familiarize yourself with a running script in your head, so it automatically rolls off your tongue when you need it but can't think of what to say.

What to Say When You Invite

It is daunting talking to someone you don't know, or someone you don't know very well! But some of the fear is pulled out of it when you keep the focus on them, and not on your fear. You have to care about them more than you care about fear. It does not matter what they think of you, it does not matter if they say no. All that matters is helping their family. Keep the focus in that place, and don't shy away from collecting no's.

I want you to work on responses to the most common rejections we get, so you always have a quick reply if someone shoots one of these at you. Then you can run off the script, and not have a panic moment being unsure of what to say. Most of these already have pre-written responses in Chapter 8 if you need a leg up! But I'd like them to be in your own words.

I am not sure I want to do this. The kit is pricey.

_____

What do I do for carpel tunnel syndrome? (Hint: DO NOT DIAGNOSE!)

_____

I'd host a class for you, but I don't have a lot of time.

_____

I like the products I'm using right now.

_____

Is this one of those network marketing things? One of those pyramid schemes?

_____

You have heard me say it before, but the key to the kit is to meet them where they are. In some conversations, you may be signing a starter kit that night. In others, they may get a drop of oil on their hand or a diffuser for the evening. In others, it may take six conversations without the word "oil" to get to the one moment where you can meet them where they are. And that's completely normal! Do not beat yourself up on the time it takes to get interest. We tend to try once, get shut down, and close down. Always keep the focus on relationships, and you are in the right place. Some will say yes, many will say no—but no now does not mean no forever!

What are the key principles to sharing oils? There are five of them! Write them down.

1) _____

2) _____

3) _____

4) _____

5) _____

What are the seven steps to the Gameplan system?

1) _____

2) _____

3) _____

4) _____

5) _____

6) _____

7) _____

CHAPTER 9

ANATOMY OF A SUCCESSFUL CLASS

What are the top three take-aways you got from the tips on how to have a successful class?

1) ....

2) ....

3) ....

Always ask yourself if what you're doing is duplicatable. Are you scaring your leaders away? Would they have to spend money on costly supplies or have gifts and talents that you posses (that they do not) to do this business?

That's one of the reasons that I don't teach out of the catalogue or the booklets that come with the Premium Starter Kit. They are fantastic, and Young Living has done an amazing job producing them. I hav them on display at every single class. But they are designed for the consumer, not the educator. That means you have to come up with the words to say. If you're very uncomfortable with speaking, that is a recipe for disaster. Stick with the 3-page script. It's designed to be read aloud. Anyone can snag it and read it on their couch.

Check off which of these activities is duplicatable:

☐ Reading the 3-page script

☐ Making Peppermint Vitality brownies or any large spread of food

☐ Using a Cricut cutter to make nice designs for Thieves bottles

☐ Going for an aromatherapy certification

☐ Touting all your wisdom and knowledge at the start of a class

☐ Making a posterboard with tons of science of oils on it

☐ Playing fun games with lots of pieces that take time to prepare

☐ Having a Premium Starter Kit on hand to pass around

☐ Showing testimony photos

☐ Having a "store" with samples that can be purchased

☐ Doing a make and take with supplies, bottles, and labels that are not on the VO

☐ Sharing the free 101 powerpoint off the oilabilityteam.com website

☐ Having a large stack of books in the front of the room where people can "do their research"

☐ Showing off oils that aren't in the starter kit (it's overwhelming to an almost-oiler)

☐ Running paid ads on Facebook (or anywhere) to promote your class

☐ Handing out folders with dozens of pages of photocopied information on oils uses

☐ Training on Savvy, Thieves, NingXia, and Seedlings in the first class (or laying out the products)

Are these things fun? Absolutely! Use them for your #ylunites rallies, events, leader's retreats, and private coaching sessions. There are only three items on that list that are duplicatable. Let's see if you found them! Keep it simple. The simpler it is, the easier it is for your leaders to copy. You don't want to scare them away with your gifts or your Young Living product stash.

Nailing the close

The close is the hardest thing to master. It's the part of the lecture where you generally feel like you're coming off salesy. But I truly want you to imagine something completely different. Your close comes down to your mindset, and nothing else. If you go into it with the goal of selling starter kits, you'll always come off salesy. If you go into it with a genuine goal of educating people and helping them to make better choices, you'll never lose.

Listen to the difference:

Starter kit mentality:

You HAVE to get the starter kit tonight. It's the best deal on Young Living's site. It's the only thing on their site that's half off. It comes with 11 bottles of oil and a diffuser. You can't get it that cheap in the store!

I do typically have a paragraph like the one above in my close. I but usually begin with something like this:

Education Mindset:

There are over 185,000 known chemicals actively used in products in the United States today. The average person puts 300 chemicals a day on their skin through 4 things: soap, shampoo, makeup and haircare. 80 of those chemicals are used before breakfast. The FDA says to date, less than 15 percent of all chemicals in the U.S. have been thoroughly studied for their side effects. Common side effects of chemical uses: endocrine disruptors, which make you gain weight, skin issues, asthma, and even cancer. There is a better way to get the poison out of your home. It comes down to making smarter decisions. What's in an oil? Lemon. Peppermint. Tangerine. Sage. No yuck. No chemicals. Nothing that will poison your body. I'd like to issue a 3-cabinet challenge: go home, pick 3 cabinets in your house, and read the ingredients that are in the products you're using. Look in your laundry room. Look under your kitchen sink and in your bathroom. If you can't pronounce it, why are you using it?

You can't control all of the toxins you'll be exposed to. But you can draw a line in the sand and say "no more" when it comes to what is found within the walls of your own home. Make a better choice today. Make the switch to oils. Oils for your deodorant instead of deodorant with aluminum. Oils in your toothpaste instead of toothpaste with fluoride. Switch out your glass cleaner and multi-surface cleaner with Thieves cleaner. Use Thieves laundry soap to get rid of your laundry soap with sodium laurel sulfate in it—known to cause cancer. There is a better way. Start with 1 small step at a time; one small swap each month. A chemical free home is a safer home.

Do you see the difference? One is in for the sale. They are on the hunt. The other is compassionately teaching. Anyone who leaves will be thinking about what's in their house. They won't be thinking you're selling to them. They'll be thinking you care about them by educating them. And if you do good follow up, you'll have another member on your team.

Take a few moments and try writing your own close to the 101 lecture. Incorporate your (FDA compliant) stories. Pull from the close above and the two closes in the back of the Gameplan book to come up with your own way to end your classes.

I'm going to have you do a bit more writing than just that. But don't stress about it—you only have to do it once, because you'll reuse it for every single class. A few sentences are enough—it need not be long.

One leader on my team told me she'd held off using my 101 Script for overtwo years, because she felt like it wasn't "hers." But when she read through this workbook and realized she could customize it, so it was in her own words with her own stories, suddenly she didn't feel as if she was relying on me to teach her classes for her. She said "just a few tweaks, and I felt like I owned it. It was amazing what my story added to the lecture. I am now confident that I'm not just reading Sarah's work to them, I am educating them—using my own story. Just a few lines made all the difference for me." (By the way, after two years of sitting on her business, in one fall, Kimarie is now an Executive, well on her way to Silver.)

For this chapter, I want you to write one paragraph that tells (compliantly) your Young Living story. Why did you get into oils? Think about that place you were at before you'd ever smelled an essential oil. Think about where you are now and the things you have learned. Show them it's one of the best choices you have made. Tell your story. Tell your why. That's how you will open your class.

For the second page, write your close. You can take one of the closing pages from the Appendix of the Gameplan book, or have your own. The most important component is that the people in the class get to smell the starter kit, and you show them where to order. Write out how you want to say it. It doesn't need to come off salesy—it can be something as simple as "I started my Young Living journey with a Premium Starter kit. That's where I'd recommend you begin, too—because you get 24% off your oils for life once you have that kit in your hands. It's the best deal out there. Let me show you how to navigate the website, for anyone wanting to sign up tonight. It takes ten minutes."

- 1—write your open. Your story.
- 2—write your close. Know your end game.

YOUR STORY.

YOUR CLOSE

CHAPTER 10

THE OIL ABILITY FOLLOW UP SYSTEM

What are the three types of people you'll encounter when you do follow up?

1) _____

2) _____

3) _____

What do you do with the people who are not interested? _____

_____

_____

What about with the people who say they can't afford it? _____

_____

_____

What are they really telling you? _____

_____

_____

Explain the Hinterkopf method of getting in touch with people after class.

_____

_____

_____

_____

How to utilize Fearless as a tool:

1) Give the little book out at classes

2) Print off the free Fearless calendar at oilabilityteam. com/fearless-tools

3) Ask for a screen shot once they have the book read and calendar filled out

4) Offer them $25 off their first Essential Rewards order (I do this either with an account credit or just mailing a $25 check)

How do you track it on your end?

I make an Excel spreadsheet of all the names that I've given the books and calendars to, whether it's been via a purple bag or in an actual class. After about five weeks goes by, I shoot them a gentle message and ask how their Fearless challenges are coming. One of two things will happen: they are nearly done, or they have not started. If they have not started, take a step back and build the relationship. They still don't see how oils will help them day to day. Meet them in their places of need and offer oils specifically for them. I don't shove Fearless down their throat. But it does do the trick in developing oilers. It gets them breaking open that box and always looking toward the next order.

Why?

The back of the book goes through the Simple Swap and breaking down room by room where the chemicals are, and how they can swap them out with Young Living products. Even item numbers are added so they can pop them right into their Essential Rewards carts. There's also a Build Your Collection page with a list of every single oil they don't own yet. They can cross them off as they build.

What is the purpose of that? It gets them always thinking toward their next order. It's about so much more than the Starter Kit. It's about the lifestyle.

Now I'm going to hold *you* accountable.

Have you read Fearless?

Have you accepted the challenges?

Are you oiling every day with intent and purpose?

Your homework assignment as you do these books is to pick up a copy of Fearless (it's on Amazon as a single copy, or in bulk, discounted, for your teams at oilabilityteam.com) and print off the calendar at oilabilityteam.com/fearless-tools, and hold yourself to the same standard. Track your orders. Be thinking about the next month and what you want to swap. It'll be so much easier to talk about it if you've done it yourself. This is a tool that WORKS. It's habit training.

- ☐ I have read Fearless
- ☐ I have filled out my Fearless calendar
- ☐ I have started using it as a duplicatable tool to train Essential Rewards and the oils lifestyle

Now...take a moment to plot out your next three Essential Rewards orders. Do this with your new oilers, too. If you give them direction, they are more likely to take action.

Month 1: Goal: 100, 190, 250, 300pv (circle one)

Simple Swap room: _____

My Essential Rewards wish list: _____

_____

_____

_____

_____

Month 2: Goal: 100, 190, 250, 300pv (circle one)

Simple Swap room: _____

My Essential Rewards wish list: _____

_____

_____

_____

_____

Month 3: Goal: 100, 190, 250, 300pv (circle one)

Simple Swap room: _____

My Essential Rewards wish list: _____

_____

_____

_____

_____

Why do I encourage 300pv orders for business builders? It's not that I want you to purchase more than you can afford. It's that you can share the product with more passion when you have had an experience with the product. When you place that order, you get the full list of free Young Living products that come with 300pv. Many of them, you may have not thought to order. As you play and build your stories around each oil, and you learn the product, you have more passion to share. It's a way of building your business to place a full 300pv order.

Not there yet? Teach classes. Share oils. Just that one simple step will build your check to the point where you can put it into your order to learn the products.

Consistency

Consistency will make or break your business. You're either sharing every week, or you have hit the pause button on your business. I want you to take a photo with your phone of your Young Living Virtual Office "OGV history" on the front page. Print it off on your printer and tape it to this page. The goal is to make it match this, because that means you're being consistent with your business:

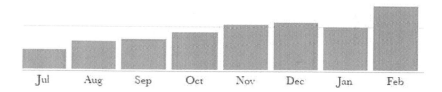

Jul   Aug   Sep   Oct   Nov   Dec   Jan   Feb

CHAPTER 11

DEALING WITH DIFFICULT PEOPLE

Give an example of enabling.

What should you do when they only want one oil?

How do you handle people who are negative about oils?

The trick is to emotionally separate yourself from the naysayers. When your identity is in what you do, you'll always have discouragement because you're basing it on performance. When your identity is in Christ, there is no pressure—because you can do all things through Christ who strengthens you. (Not a few things, all things.) Nothing is impossible. That means you kick the dust off your feet at each no, don't wear it as a discouragement, and move on.

YOUR ASSIGNMENT: CHANGE YOUR ATTITUDE

As you go through your week, try to put this into practice. Write down an example (it may not even be oils related) where you were able to walk away from conflict with a positive attitude.

BONUS ASSIGNMENT: BECOME A CONFIDENT ENTREPRENEUR

Do you need a little more science behind the decision to do network marketing? Do you need a little more convincing? Go to ericworre.com and pick up his "Rise of the Entrepreneur" DVD. It's 50 minutes long, and jam-packed with fact-filled science on this profession. If you're ever worried about where it goes, don't be. The stats don't lie. Just put one foot in front of the other, despite the naysayers, knowing what you are doing will bless your family. As long as you believe this is possible, it is.

CHAPTER 12

NO ONE IS COMING TO CLASSES- NOW WHAT?

Because everyone in the world needs oils, each person has an average friend circle of 2,000 people, and there are thousands of Silvers and above with the same skill set and resources that you have, I'd say the issue is not who you know or your resources. The issue is how people are perceiving you.

YOUR ASSIGNMENT: CHANGE YOUR PERCEPTION

I want to run you through a quick exercise. I know I already made you read the 101 Script 10 times, but I want you to read it through one more time. At least read the first paragraph.

For the first time through, just do a quick dry read. Read it as though you're giving it at class tonight.

Now I'm going to take you through a visual exercise. I want you to imagine that you are a Young Living Royal Crown Diamond. On the 20th this month, $245,000 will be deposited into your bank account. You are debt free. Your family members and closest friends are cared for. You give generously. You are living comfortably. And you've had that income for 10 years. Next month, another $275,000 will be deposited into your account!

Would you carry yourself differently? Would you have more confidence? Would you treat people with more grace or live on the ragged edge? Would you be well rested? Would you take care of your body? Would you set aside more time for family and friends? Would you live in fear? Would you be afraid of the future?

I want you to live as though you're already there. Envision yourself in that place. Speak with confidence. Hold your head high, because you did the grunt work to earn that rank. Nothing was handed to you. You know what it takes to run a multi-million-dollar network marketing business.

Now go read the first paragraph of your 101 lecture. Read it like you've sold 1000 starter kits. Read it like everyone says yes and everyone respects what you have to say.

THAT is how you should read that lecture.

One other tactic I want to give you is the Eric Worre "If I, will you" principle. It's fantastic, and Worre is a network marketing genius.

Don't ever hand things out to people without expecting something in return. I use this principle all the time with my business builders. You'll notice in the back of Gameplan there is Teacher Training guide on how to raise leaders. I have personally trained over 800 leaders in one year with that system. There are seven homework assignments they must complete (which takes them through one full cycle of a Young Living business: marketing, filling classes, teaching, and follow up). Only then can they earn more materials from me to grow their business. (I personally recommend you give them the Gameplan book and workbook as a reward, but I am biased...) Here's how I use the "If I, will you" tactic with my leaders:

"If I give you 7 homework assignments in exchange for a Gameplan book and workbook, will you complete them?"

It really weeds out the people who say they will do something from the people who actually get out there and do it. You are one of those people who actually gets out there and does it, because you've made it halfway through the workbook and Gameplan, the hardest Young Living strategy book out there.

Here's another example of "If I, will you?"

"If I give you this 101 lecture on audio cd, will you listen to it in your car?"

Now you practice writing an "if I will you" statement, based on something you would hand out.

Great job! The last step to that trick is following up. Set a date where you can check in and make sure they actually did the work. Then if you're looking to sell a starter kit, that's the time to approach them with your close or with getting to a 101 lecture in a live class.

The Skill of Storytelling

This is one of my favorite quotes from the Gameplan book: "one of the biggest traps in network marketing is believing that if you just shove enough facts at people, they will eventually change their minds and buy in to whatever you are selling. But scientists have proven that we make decisions based on emotion, not information."

You do that by telling your story. I am not talking about the open or close to your class, I'm talking about those random chance conversations when people ask you what you're wearing—or show slight interest in any oils product. You have to have your story down, and deliver it in a tight, convincing package—with passion.

Here are some questions I want you to answer as you craft your own personal story:

1) How did an oil touch your family? (You can still tell this compliantly!)

2) What has been your experience with the Thieves line, and chemical free living?

3) How did you get your starter kit—what prompted you to begin?

4) What has happened to your family and the way you view wellness since then?

Come up with a three or four sentence "story" of your introduction to oils, and why you love them so much, below, by answering the questions:

_____

_____

_____

_____

Now we're going to take this a step further. I want you to come up with a personal story for each item in the Premium Starter Kit. Just give a few bullet point words to remind yourself of the experience you've had with each of these products. If you haven't had an experience yet, look up their uses in the Life Science Desk Reference (pocket edition works well!) and start applying them in those ways so you can build a story. Be deliberate about your personal oils use, and then it is fair to place that expectation on your new oilers, too.

DiGize: _____

_____

Thieves: _____

_____

Copaiba: _____

_____

Lemon: _____

_____

Peppermint: _____

_____

Stress Away: _____

_____

Raven: _____

_____

Frankincense: _____

_____

Citrus Fresh: _____

_____

Pan Away: _____

_____

Lavender: _____

_____

Desert Mist (or any of the Young Living diffusers): _____

_____

Thieves cleaning sample: _____

_____

NingXia Red: _____

_____

The Skill of Speaking Life: Mindset Training

Make a list of all the things you believe about your business right now. I want you to be completely honest! It's just between you and you, no one else will see.

Do you have beliefs such as:
> I can't fill classes.
> I can't find leaders.
> I can't seem to get my OGV to move.
> No one will sign up for Essential Rewards.
> All my leaders move SLOW.
> No one will come to my rallies or events.
> I will never git Diamond.

Take a moment and write down the ones that hit you most, or come up with new ones, and I want you to write the OPPOSITE below. Then copy it again on a Post It note and put it somewhere where you can see it every single day. Here's the reality: when you speak those words over your business, you are cursing it. Speak LIFE every single day. Scripture says "death and life are in the power of the tongue." Proverbs 18:21. You are causing death to your business with the simple act of speaking these words aloud. So speak the opposite instead, and you'll start to believe it—and you'll move.

Make your list: _____

_____

_____

_____

_____

_____

_____

_____

What are the 3 skills you need to master to get to Diamond?

1) _____

_____

_____

2) _____

_____

_____

3) _____

_____

_____

BONUS STRATEGY: HOW TO CONQUER A PLATEAU

There are two other tactics to try if you are having a hard time getting people to class.

Tactic number one: One on one's

Go back to that list of all the people you know, and sit down with them, one or two a week, and start signing people up by meeting with them alone over lunch or dinner. It's amazing how this can help your morale when you plateau. Just keep at it. Never give up.

Those relationships will lead to open doors that explode your business later. You never know who that one person is that ends up being a Diamond beneath you. How do you do a one-on-one? Exactly the same way you do a class with 15 people in it. Grab the 3-page 101 lecture, and read it. Do good follow up. When you touch base, ask if they are willing to host with their friend circle. And watch it grow. My sister had to do one-on-ones for the first 9 months of her business. She had moved to New York from Chicago and had no friend circle because she was working 3 jobs—80 hours a week. She had no personal time to develop relationships, so for months, she used her lunch break for one-on-one's. She eventually signed enough people that she developed a friend circle through their circles. She's now a Silver in Six, and two-thirds of the way to Gold. Keep at it, and never give up. The only thing that kills your business is not doing anything with your business.

Tactic number two: Vendor Events

This is a great way to generate leads. Why isn't a great way to sell kits? Because the average person at a vendor booth will spend less than 60 seconds at your booth as they are perusing. It's really hard to get the enthusiasm going to make a purchase in under 60 seconds. But vendor events are gold if you have no friend circle, because they generate leads. A lead is a person who might come to or host a class.

Here are a few extra pointers in addition to the vendor event tips in Gameplan:

–have your starter kit front and center, right smack dab in the middle of the booth, eye level. Use levels (like $10 crates) to get it right in front of their face. You don't want anyone walking away without the smell of an oil in their nose.

–make sure you have a collection system. It's critical you're collecting their information to generate interest in classes. If you don't have this, you have just wasted your time at the event. I usually do this by offering an oils gift basket as a raffle, and collecting people's names on clipboards to win it. If you want the sign up sheet I place on the clipboard, check out the Appendix on Vendor Events in the Gameplan book.

–it's critical that you have some type of a 30-second script memorized. It's the spiel that you give each person that comes to the booth. You will say it three hundred times a day at a vendor event—the exact same paragraph. It should tell them:

- □ what oils are
- □ why they want them in their life
- □ where they can start

If you need an idea of how to put that together, my vendor script looks something like this:

Hi there! My name is _____. I'm a Young Living essential oils distributor. Essential oils are used for cleaning, personal care products, supplements, to get chemicals out of the home, and to support systems in the body. What does that mean? I would never go a winter without RC in my diffuser during cold and flu season—it's wonderful for respiratory support. Peppermint is the first thing I apply when my stomach feels off—it's a digestive system support oil. Many people buy the kit for Pan Away alone. You will love it on your muscles! I started my Young Living journey with a starter kit. It's the best place to begin because it's the only thing on Young Living's site that's half off. Once you have a kit, every oil for life is 24 percent off. No membership fees. No yearly fee. It's the best choice I made for my family this year. Here's how to learn more...

BAM.

Then...

–make sure they have a tool. If you can afford it, depending on how big the vendor event is. I like to hand off flyers to everyone with information on how to order and my business card, and for some, my audio cd's. It's a lecture they can tune into in their car on the way home.

Now follow up. When you leave that event, look at every person who said they were interested in learning more and make contact with them. This is where the goldmine part comes in. See if they'll get two non-oilers to come with them to meet you for coffee or dinner—and you're off and running. You now have a new friend circle.

CHAPTER 13

KEYS TO CONFIDENCE

What are the reasons that you lack confidence? Nail down your root cause.

_____

_____

Did God make you that way?

_____

This is the fork in the road for you for this business. For you to be successful from here on out, you have a big decision to make. You have to decide that your desire to be successful is greater than your fear of failure. This is where you really have to make the decision that you want it. For some people, that decision, conscious and spoken aloud, is enough for them to move on and knock this out of the ballpark.

For others, it takes a bit more. The emotional abuse runs deep. The pain from the past is raw. The walls built around them are high. The experiences they have had lead them to believe they are not good, not worth it, not believable. The thing is, if you believe that about yourself, you emulate that to the people around you. And here's the thing: IT'S NOT TRUE. God made no mistakes when He made you. His plan is totally perfect. So you can stay where you are and keep believing lies, or you can take steps to get out from the place you have been living and fly. You were created to help other people. If you live in emotional bondage, you can't pour into anyone.

YOUR ASSIGNMENT: TAKE STEPS TOWARD CONFIDENCE

If you're in that place, do me a favor. Go to danijohnson.com and just look at one of her First Steps to Success seminars. It's a chunk of change for a weekend. But I've had dozens and dozens of my team members go through the training, and never once have any of them said it wasn't worth it financially. Please hear my heart, leader. This truly is not me trying to sell you something. I have absolutely nothing to gain from you going. But I am that confident that it will be a game changer for you emotionally. If your barrier is your confidence, this will be the best investment you make in your business. If you can't get people to attend your classes—and you have tried all my tips in this book—you NEED to get to Dani Johnson.

John's and my OGV was 46,000 when we first went. Five months later, it was 152,000. It's because she helps you get rid of the emotional baggage that's keep you from connecting with people. If you lack confidence, if you make excuses, if you are in a rut, if you have plateaued, if you can't get people to class, if you feel overwhelmed, you should be at her training. And you should get your leaders there. The more leaders you get there, the faster you will grow. I took 30 leaders my next Dani event and our OGV spiked to 185,000 this fall. Our pace is now 245,000 OGV before Christmas. If this is the turning point for you, write down the date you're going to Dani and make no excuses. Just get there.

Date I am going to Dani: _____

Current OGV: _____

Date I went to Dani: _____

OGV 6 months later: _____

If you think you have this business nailed on your own, it's time to start walking, talking, and thinking like a Diamond—and holding classes and training leaders like one. You were made to pour into the people around you. But you have to be in a place to pour. If you're always running on empty, it's time to figure out why and change it.

Make a list of some of the "train your brain" products you would like to try. Make it a point to get one of them in your head each week. Check them off as you complete them!

☐ _____

☐ _____

☐ _____

☐ _____

☐ _____

CHAPTER 14

YOUR BUSINESS TOOLKIT: OILY TOOLS, TAXBOT, AND MORE

This is a very simple workbook chapter to write, because I want you to pick up the resources in this chapter and start to utilize them. They make everything else easier.

Oily Tools

Go to the app store, download it to your cell phone, and pay $7 a month for the program. It's genius. Not only can you see your paycheck projected by rank, you can also see your pace OGV (where the program believes you'll end up at the end of the month.) This has been one of the biggest motivators for me to keep going in my Young Living business. It's the best $7 dollars I spent outside my starter kit.

Taxbot.

Go online and pay for the program. It's $5 a month for Young Living distributors. You can track your mileage from your cell phone and it automatically uploads. It also connects with your bank and lets you know when receipts need to be scanned in for charges to be reconciled. It makes taxes easy. And that's saying a lot. You can get 50 percent off Taxbot each month ($5 instead of $10) by using this link: https://taxbot.com/z/yl/

While we are on the topic of paychecks and taxes, may I freely offer some advice? I am a big proponent on living on less then you make. Being a millionaire won't help you if you're spending more than a million dollars. John and I draw up a business budget every single month based on my checks. You can do this, too, if your check is 50 dollars or 50,000 dollars.

A family business typically in the United States doesn't see a profit until year seven. In Young Living, I saw a profit on month one. My very first paycheck was $340, twice what I spent on my starter kit. I paid my husband back for the kit, ordered business cards, and placed my Essential Rewards order with that first check, and stayed totally debt free. All you need to launch your business is a starter kit and a 101 Script.

When I first started, all the cash from my business went right back into my business. When I retired a year after I got my kit, I set aside a portion of my check for debt to cover what my anchoring income had covered, but most still went to my business. When my husband retires on Labor Day this year, 2 years out from getting our kit, then this outline will look a bit different. For the purpose of writing a starter kit to Silver book, most generally aren't retired yet and using their Young Living income for their personal finances. If you put it back into the business, it will grow your business. In Gameplan 2, look for our new budget, with our family finances mixed in.

This is how I delegate my paycheck right now. Our income is about $10,000 a month, but I base it on our lowest check over the past six months, $7,600. If I have extra, it goes to tithe, debt, or savings.

10% tithe	$760
20% taxes	$1520
20% debt	$1520
12% payroll	$912

(I pay my kids to help me at classes, and have a personal assistant to help with mailings. She works about 15 hours a month.) If you don't need this category, add it to debt

5% Essential Rewards	$380 (SWEET!)
15% gas and food	$1140

(I use this to get to classes, and also help with our budget)

10% Young Living expenses	$760

If you have a NingXia bar at classes, or order samples or flyers)

4% travel	$304
4% awards and recognition on my team	$304

That's what my business budget looks like right now. Each month my check changes, and I just adjust it to the ratios above. It works! I saved all the money for my taxes, gave generously, paid a lot of debt, had the income to visit and train and recognize leaders, and cover my essential rewards order.

Gameplanner

This planner was put together after over a year of research and study of hundreds of other planning systems. This is the glue that makes the entire Gameplan system stick for your business. It will keep you laser focused on teaching classes, getting people on Essential Rewards, and training your leaders.

Books.

Oh my. I could give you 100 different books to read. That's probably one of the top things I get asked by my team- "what are you reading this week, Sarah?". About every other week someone asks me to post my current reading list, and it usually has at least 30 books on it. Since I'm used to reading 39 newspapers each morning to write news the past 18 years, I read a lot. I believe if you're not reading, you're not growing. It's a way to pour into you. If you are about to finish Gameplan and you truly want to keep growing in your network marketing awesomeness, I am working on a 7-week Rise to Silver bootcamp: Gameplan Edition that will kick your tush. It's 35 hours of intense videos and intimate training. You can do it on your own or in a small group. You'll be able to find it at oilabilityteam.com (This is only for over achievers!) I have also hinted that I'm working on a Gameplan II—which will be for Silvers and above.

If you want a little less work because frankly, this book knocked you flat out and set you into full-on adrenal fatigue, here are my favorite from-the-hammock reads:

- Eric Worre's Go Pro
- Eric Worre's Rise of the Entrepreneur DVD
- Dale Carnegie's How To Win Friends and Influence People
- My favorite book on aromatherapy is still Dr. David Stewart's Healing Oils of the Bible.
- The Essential Oil Truth Second Edition: the Facts Without the Hype by Jen O'Sullivan
- French Aromatherapy: Essential Oil Recipes & Usage Guide by Jen O'Sullivan
- Living Balanced: Healthy Mind & Body Reference Guide by Stacey Kimbrell

Just remember: don't get so caught up in learning and education that you're not out there teaching classes. When your classes suffer, it's time to cut back. I pretty much only read when I cannot do anything else: when I'm in an airplane, when I'm in a hotel, when I'm waiting for a kid to get out of Boy Scouts or ballet.

YOUR ASSIGNMENT: GET YOUR TOOLS

This is a four part assignment, covering each of the key areas of a well-organized business.

1. If you love reading and want to continue to grow, make a list of 3 books you'd like to check out yourself, pick a copy up and have at it.

   ☐ _____

   ☐ _____

   ☐ _____

2. Draw up a rough draft of your budget, where you'd like to see your pennies go from this business. Then for 30 days, track all your spending and see where it goes. See if you can stick to the percentages you have written down.

My Young Living Budget:

_____ % _____
_____ % _____
_____ % _____
_____ % _____
_____ % _____
_____ % _____
_____ % _____
_____ % _____
_____ % _____
_____ % _____

3. Pick up a planner and start using it. Track your mileage. Write down your classes. Prep for next month.

4. At least check out Taxbot and Oily Tools. Purchase them when you see you have the money in your business budget. You'll be glad you did.

CHAPTER 15

GROWING YOUR BUSINESS ONLINE

This is the only chapter that you get a get-out-of-jail-for-free pass. If you truly are not a writer, you can skip the blogging advice and I promise I will not hunt you down. The dog has eaten your homework and you are forgiven.

There are those of you who believe you have a writing talent, but truly, your writing is depressing. It's ok. I am not good at math. You really don't want to see me doing Calculus—I get to the point where I'm throwing the book at the wall. If you think you have talent but everyone around you says it's just not so, you, too, may skip this chapter. In fact, please skip it. I am asking in the name of all the people out there who do technical editing for a living.

Word of caution on blogging: don't try to launch your Young Living business with a skill you have not mastered yet. If you've never run a blog, don't assume that's your ticket to Diamond with Young Living. It takes a lot of skill to run a blog. You have to understand the inner workings of WordPress, or whatever blogging site you're using as your platform, you have to be a strong writer, and you have to know how to build a list. I'd rather see you grab the three-page script and get it in front of people on your couch then spend a year trying to learn to blog. That's a year that you could be having a Gold or Platinum paycheck, if only you'd start. If you are already a blogger and have the skill, by all means—go for it. But don't use blogging as your get-rich-quick scheme. It's a lot harder than it looks.

For the Bloggers

If you are in the minority that have both the writing skills and technical aptitude, go ahead and give blogging a try. I'd encourage you to go to Wordpress and try knocking out your own blog. Get 10 posts up before you make it live so there is some content on the sight.

These are the steps to launching a blog:

1. Choose a name
2. Choose a hosting company
3. Choose a domain name (ours is oilabilityteam.com)
4. Choose a logo
5. Set up your page on Wordpress

And you are off and running!

Training and Growing on Facebook

Facebook is simply a tool. It's a mechanism for you to connect with a LOT of people in a very short period of time, with minimal skill required.

Write down the nine things you need to utilize Facebook well:

_____

_____

_____

_____

_____

Now let's put it into action. (It's ok! You can do it!) Tell your team you're doing your first Facebook Live. Get a 3x5 card and bulletpoint three topics you want to discuss. (Not sure what to pick? Go through the Gameplan book! Start with Chapter 1 or 2, and cover one topic a week). Make sure you write down your open and your close, so you know how to start and how to get out of it. Have good lighting and a smile—and you're off. If you can get into the habit of doing these once a week at a time when your team can get on, you'll build a larger and larger audience with each Live.

Cross off the box for the first 12 Lives you do... by three months, you have this DOWN!

☐ ☐ ☐ ☐ ☐ ☐ ☐ ☐ ☐ ☐ ☐ ☐

YOUR ASSIGNMENT: UPDATE YOUR SOCIAL MEDIA PROFILES

You may never be a blogger, but I bet you have a Facebook profile, an Instagram identity, or Twitter account! Make sure people who already follow you know that you love the oils and that you can help educate them. For those of us that truly have no talent to create a blog or website, you can still have a rockstar social media presence. Start with whatever platforms you're already on.

1. Update your profile to include that you are with Young Living.

2. Use the tips in Chapter 15 to share short, enthusiastic, compliant posts alongside whatever else you share online.

Don't hide the fact that you're an oiler. People do business with those they know, like and trust. They may be interested in oils, but want to learn from a friend—and that friend could be you! I have sold two kits simply by people checking out my profiles. We can share oils online just by putting 140 characters onto Twitter about our son's stinky shoes. It's possible! So start there.

And if you have no gift, stay far, far away from Wordpress.

Let me repeat that: far away. It falls under the 'distractions' category for you.

CHAPTER 16

STAYING LEGAL: COMPREHENSIVE FDA TRAINING

Write down 10 things you're not allowed to do:

1) _____

2) _____

3) _____

4) _____

5) _____

6) _____

7) _____

8) _____

9) _____

10 _____

I tell people if you're not sure if it's legal, just think of what is on the shelves at Walgreens. If an item is sold in that store, it's likely FDA approved. You can't talk about your oils like you would about any item at a drug store. That means no bug spray or sunscreen. It also means the FDA is looking for intent. You can't market "sun spray"—or they'll be on to you. Run your business with integrity. Let people do their own research on the oils. Don't make things up illicitly and don't try to skirt around the rules.

Why does the FDA put limits on what you can say about oils? _____

Why doesn't Young Living just become FDA approved? You tell me below.

YOUR ASSIGNMENT: EQUIP, DON'T PRESCRIBE

The moral of the chapter: teach people how to fish instead of giving them fish. What are some resources you can give them to start their own research? List 2.

CHAPTER 17

THE YOUNG LIVING COMPENSATION PLAN, IN LAYMAN'S TERMS

This is where it gets tricky! Who REALLY understands the comp plan? I have a little secret for you. You don't need to. It's completely broken down for you in the Virtual Office under "my account". Just look up your commissions check, click on each item (Unilevel, starter kit bonuses, etc.), and you can see exactly who you were paid on, and how much. It's actually quite fun to see it all broken down.

It's not bad to have a basic understanding though. Tell me what each of the four things below are:

Starter Kit bonuses: _____

_____

Fast Start: _____

_____

Unilevel: _____

_____

Rising Star and Generation Leadership Bonuses: _____

_____

On what day of the month are you paid? _____

Now write down a goal. What do you want your paycheck to be six months from now? _____

This may sound a little silly, but it really helps to visualize where you want to be. I want you to take a check out of your checkbook, sign Mary Young's name to it, and fill it out for where you'd like to see your Young Living monthly paycheck—one year from today. Then tape it right in this workbook under this paragraph. When you hit benchmarks, write them down next to the check, and the date you hit it. It's incredible the places you will go when you can see in your head where you want to end up. It's like following the basketball as you throw it through the air, or watching the hoop where you want it to go. It's much more likely to go in if your eyes are on the hoop. Fill out a check, tape in on this page, and keep your eyes on the hoop.

What rank do you want to be THIS YEAR? _____

Let's break it down into smaller goals to help you get to that paycheck. For me, John and I have a goal of Diamond. We're about 100,000 OGV down and 2 of our 5 legs are about 5-thousand OGV short. So my goals look like this:

Month 1: Increase 2 legs OGV by 1500 each, to 11,500

25,000 OGV growth

Month 2: Increase 2 legs OGV by 1500 each, to 13,000

25,000 OGV growth

Month 3: Increase 2 legs OGV by 1500 each, to 14,500

25,000 OGV growth

Month 4: Increase 2 legs the last 500

25,000 OGV growth

Now what do I need to do to attain those goals? First, I need to be strategic. I may be getting requests to teach on my other 3 legs, but for a season, I have to laser hone in on the two legs that are too low to rank. So for 4 months, all of my classes must be under a person on one of those two legs. I won't get distracted. I focus solely on them to get to the goal.

What about OGV growth? 25,000 OGV is a lot to grow in 1 month, even for a Platinum. How do I attain that? My husband and I did some brainstorming on how to grow OGV, and we leaned on the wisdom of the Diamonds before us. I asked the what worked and what didn't work. I got a few tips.

How to Increase OGV

Get as many people as you can to convention (so we incentivized our team with swag bags and got 30 people there this year, 10 times more than last year)

Get as many people as you can to Dani Johnson training to get rid of emotional blocks holding them back from ranking (we were able to get 27 people there this year)

Do a Silver bootcamp. I recommend the resources at oilabilityteam. com. Do you know the Gameplan book and workbook were designed to be used in a small group format? You can go on Facebook Live or Zoom and take a chapter a week and do it with your leaders. At that rate, with

24 chapters, it would either take you 6 months, or you could meet for 30 minutes a night for 24 straight days and do a 5-week bootcamp. Option 3 is to simply take the 3-page leader training in the back of Gameplan and break it out into a week of intense training with vision boards, the Rise of the Entrepreneur DVD, and accountability and incentives.

Consider contests and awards. Our team goes CRAZY for them. We do them within our budget, but we have something special set aside each month, even if it's just an hour of coaching with me.

Launch a Facebook page where everyone in the business can grow together and are on the same page for encouragement and leadership.

Do a weekly Facebook live or Zoom chat for leadership training.

To increase our OGV by 100,000, our team needs to sell 1,000 kits. If I break that over 4 months, that's 250 kits a month. Our average team wide is 200 kits a month. I'm setting a goal of 250 kits a month plus 30 new people on Essential Rewards to maintain the volume. I'll give awards for kit sales or Essential Rewards sign ups.

Do you see how I laid out tangible, doable goals?

Let's walk you through process now, so you can work on ranking yourself.

Rank Mapping

I am going to include a little bonus for workbook users only in this section. It is something I have done since I realized I was running a Young Living business, and it's something I recommend that you do, too. It's called Rank Mapping. Basically, you are plotting out your goals so you know how far you are away from your next rank. This doesn't work well if you're a Star trying to plot your way to Royal Crown Diamond. But for each individual rank advancement, it's amazing. It will really help you if you want to work the Elite Express program and hit certain ranks within certain benchmarks.

First, plot out what rank you are going for. How much OGV do you need overall, and how much are you short? Second, break it down by leg. Then, break it down by classes (this is an estimate). Then, look at the people you have on that specific leg that have sold kits, and work closely with them. Work with the people that are working. If you need 4,000 OGV, and you have 3,300 OGV, then you're 700 short. 700 = 7 starter kits = 2-3 classes, if you average two kits per class.

This is what it looks like. If you want to go even deeper, pick up the Gameplanner and it will walk you through rank mapping month by month.

Current OGV: _____ OGV Goal: _____ OGV Needed: _____

Leg 1: Current OGV: _____ OGV Goal: _____

OGV Needed: _____ Classes: _____

Leg 2: Current OGV: _____ OGV Goal: _____

OGV Needed: _____ Classes: _____

Leg 3: Current OGV: _____ OGV Goal: _____

OGV Needed: _____ Classes: _____

Leg 4: Current OGV: _____ OGV Goal: _____

OGV Needed: _____ Classes: _____

Leg 5: Current OGV: _____ OGV Goal: _____

OGV Needed: _____ Classes: _____

Leg 6: Current OGV: _____ OGV Goal: _____

OGV Needed: _____ Classes: _____

Now make a list of everyone on your weak leg that has sold a kit. Work with them. Train them on Gameplan. Train them on purple bags. Get them teaching one class a week and doing follow up at the end of each month. Your greatest business tool in Young Living is the power of duplication.

List of leaders on my weak leg: _____

_____

YOUR ASSIGNMENT: MAKE SPECIFIC GOALS

What is your desired rank? _____

How many months do you want to take to get there? _____

What do you have to do for OGV and for your legs to attain that rank?

_____

_____

What tactics do you think will work to specifically increase OGV and work on those legs? _____

_____

_____

Make a list of goals you can work on each month to get where you want to be:

Month 1: _____

Month 2: _____

Month 3: _____

Month 4: _____

Month 5: _____

Month 6: _____

Here's one word of caution. Be diligent. And be focused. If you lose your focus, you'll lose your goal. Lay boundaries while you're working on rank, and stick closely with the goals you have laid out. And you will get there.

CHAPTER 18

A Young Living Strategy Guide On Where to Sign New Oilers

Which strategy will you use—Focused on Silver, or Rising Star? Neither is wrong!

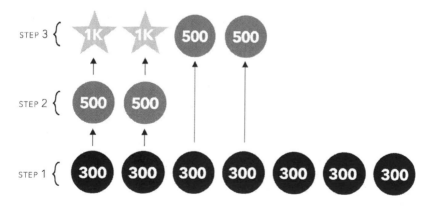

There are only two mistakes you can make when structuring your business:

Building too _____ and building too _____

Take a moment in the box below and plot out what your strategy will look like. Who are your legs? How much OGV do you need in each to get them to where they need to be to rank up? Draw a visual sketch of your goals.

When you are teaching for someone else on your team, who should get the check—you, or them? _____

Why? _____

_____

What is sponsor? _____

What is enroller?_____

Can you be the sponsor and someone under you be the enroller? __

Why or why not? _____

_____

How can you remember which is which? E comes before

YOUR ASSIGNMENT: IDENTIFY YOUR LEGS

Write down the names of two people you think may have the potential to be business builders:

As a backup, write down the names of two people you believe would order 100PV a month, or you'd just truly like to see blessed:

This week... talk to them.

_____

CHAPTER 19

The Key to Reaching and Maintaining Rank

Come up with a strategy for your follow up. (But in the same breath, don't overdo it.) I'll give someone a couple of mailings and several conversations before I stop pressing hard on Essential Rewards. I do not mail a non-oiler a package every single month for a year. At that point, it's much more important that you build the relationship over spending your entire Young Living check at the post office.

Write out a schedule of what your mailings would look like. I recommend training the lifestyle first, with Fearless and the Fearless calendar.

Month 1: _____

_____

Month 2: _____

_____

Month 3: _____

_____

Month 4: _____

_____

Month 5: _____

_____

Month 6: _____

_____

Why is Essential Rewards critical? _____

_____

_____

Can you wait until you're a Silver to start signing people up for Essential Rewards? _____

Tell me why. _____

_____

_____

YOUR ASSIGNMENT: CREATE YOUR ESSENTIAL REWARDS PACKAGE

Each person has a different system to putting together mailings (or "care packages")—for their new members. Take a photo of one of your care packages and tape it right here—in this book. It'll give you a giggle in two or three years as you get better and better with them, to see the things you included when you first began. When I first started, it was usually a business card and a flyer. Now it's Cool Azul pain cream, a sample of Thieves cleaner, or something very practical that they can try out. I also love to give my audio lectures on CD to them, to start to train them how important it is to use oils over chemicals.

Place your photo here:

Whatever you decide to include, each package must have a purpose. It needs to explain Essential Rewards, or no one will be signing up for ER. They need to have ideas of what to order, because they're entirely new to oils. They need to understand the promos for that month, because they likely will spend a bit more to hit a benchmark. So every package I send out at least has those three items in it, plus a few extras.

CHAPTER 20

BALANCE, BOUNDARIES, AND TREATING YOUR BUSINESS AS A BUSINESS

Are you an overscheduler?

If you are not, you have permission to skip this chapter too. (Look at that! I gave a free pass for 2 chapters!!!) If you are, I have yet another reading list for you. (After this workbook, of course!) These are my favorite reads for how to balance the business alongside your own life. You don't want your kids eating cereal and apples and cheese for six months while you build to Silver, and you don't want it to take 18 years to rank, so how do you do it all? How do you fit it in one 24-hour day?

These were the books I digested. Order them and put a check mark next to them as you finish them. You must learn to manage your time wisely. I assure you—it can be done. It just takes self-control and discipline.

☐ Start with Dani's training series on time management, Time Secrets.

☐ Lisa Terkeursts' "The Best Yes"

☐ Dr. Henry Cloud and Dr. John Townsend's "Boundaries"

As you wait for those to arrive, there are a few practical things we can do to help you lay out a Gameplan for how to get Young Living in your day.

Budget your day out.

Literally.

Take the next few lines, and write out when you'd set aside time to do your business. Leave time for follow up, mailings, and leadership training. Then pop in some classes, too. And let's see what the layout of your week would look like.

MONDAY

7:00 am
8:00 am
9:00 am
10:00 am
11:00 am
12:00 pm
1:00 pm
2:00 pm
3:00 pm
4:00 pm
5:00 pm
6:00 pm
7:00 pm
8:00 pm
9:00 pm

TUESDAY

7:00 am
8:00 am
9:00 am
10:00 am
11:00 am
12:00 pm
1:00 pm
2:00 pm
3:00 pm
4:00 pm
5:00 pm
6:00 pm
7:00 pm
8:00 pm
9:00 pm

WEDNESDAY

7:00 am
8:00 am
9:00 am
10:00 am
11:00 am
12:00 pm
1:00 pm
2:00 pm
3:00 pm
4:00 pm
5:00 pm
6:00 pm
7:00 pm
8:00 pm
9:00 pm

THURSDAY

7:00 am
8:00 am
9:00 am
10:00 am
11:00 am
12:00 pm
1:00 pm
2:00 pm
3:00 pm
4:00 pm
5:00 pm
6:00 pm
7:00 pm
8:00 pm
9:00 pm

FRIDAY

7:00 am
8:00 am
9:00 am
10:00 am
11:00 am
12:00 pm
1:00 pm
2:00 pm
3:00 pm
4:00 pm
5:00 pm
6:00 pm
7:00 pm
8:00 pm
9:00 pm

SATURDAY

7:00 am
8:00 am
9:00 am
10:00 am
11:00 am
12:00 pm
1:00 pm
2:00 pm
3:00 pm
4:00 pm
5:00 pm
6:00 pm
7:00 pm
8:00 pm
9:00 pm

Now do it. Hold yourself to a clock and make it happen. Cut out the distractions sucking your time from accomplishing your goal. If you have a goal of 1 hour a day, make it happen. If it's 30 minutes, that's 30 minutes you're not spending right now. It all comes down to your diligence. You have to stop when the clock switches to the next hour. Make sure your priorities are in line, and you've got time set aside for the things that matter most.

If you are a homeschooler, or if you just need some more balance to keep your home clean and you have a couple of kids, there was a wonderful book (with charts to fill in and hang on the wall) that I use a lot in my home. You can find it at titus2ministries.com

Look for: "Managers of their Chores". "Managers of their Homes" is also good. A second resources is the Accountable Kids set if you are having a hard time getting your kids to help you out with the house. Find info on that at accountablekids.com

As for "Managers of their Chores", I use the same charts in that book to lay out my day. It's literally just a grid, broken into 30 minute or 1 hour increments. And it works!

Now when it comes time to actually fill that hour of business time with work, what do you do?

One of the downsides to running your own business is that the work is never finished. You never get to a place where you feel like you've arrived and you can just walk away. In news, once I shut off my mic, I went home and didn't think about news for about 18 hours. It was wonderful. I was fully engaged in homeschooling. But with a home-based business, you always have a to-do list.

How do you get around the always-behind feeling? Shorten your list. Make it manageable. I'm going to tell you about a simple exercise you can do right when you wake up—one that will get more and more practical as your team grows—because I'll tell you, managing 3200 people can take a lot out of you some days! You bounce from leader to leader and fire to fire on some days, and excitement and joy and jubilation in 40 places other days. Time management is critical the larger you grow!

As you rise, think about your day—and what the absolutely most important things of your business are. It may be helping a member move someone by a deadline, or changing someone's Essential Reward's order before it goes through, or setting up your classes so you can market them for the next 2 weeks. Whatever the 3 most important things are, those go on your list—and you don't beat yourself up if you feel there are 5 more things that should go on it, but that you never get to.

Put those items in order of importance. And I don't do anything else (during your business work time) until those items are done first.

Our Diamond, Jay Carter, has a slightly different approach. He actually makes a list of 7 things—but it includes personal items like working out, getting in the Word, and making food or cleaning. After 7 items, his day is done and he has the liberty to rest. It's wonderful.

YOUR ASSIGNMENT: MAKE YOUR LIST OF THREE

Starting today—right now—make a list of the three things you'd like to do today. And keep the list manageable—if you only have an hour, don't write "read the whole Gameplan book."

1) ....

2) ....

3) ....

Try those tactics when budgeting out your work day.

Treat each day as a true work day, too. When I am getting ready to work on Young Living business, I will change out of my sweatpants. I may put a little makeup on.

I set aside time and the kids know they are not to interrupt me—it's the same as if I'm in the anchor chair. It's my time. They use that time to work quietly on their work or their readers, or they get extra chores. Establish a sense of importance around the family business. But when it's time to shut it off, focus on them.

Have an end time each day, so your kids know it's not all-consuming. When we are homeschooling, my phone is shut off. They have all my attention. When we're outside playing laser tag as a family, I'm not taking business calls. I have set business hours that are respected both by my team and by my family. And family time is respected by John and I. No business.

Try sticking to your business schedule this week and see how much you accomplish and how balanced you feel!

CHAPTER 21

FINDING AND RAISING LEADERS

This is probably the simplest chapter to write for the workbook. I want you to go to the Appendix in Gameplan, grab the "Teacher Training: How to Launch Yong Living Leaders" section, and get in front of a mirror and read it. Then go practice it on your mom.

Then every time you see a little plus sign in your organization next to a name in "my organization" in the Virtual Office, it means someone has sold a kit. They need to be trained. In month 2 of my business, I had 27 different people share a kit. Most of them have now dropped off my team because I never took the time to train them on how to get their oils for free. Take that 3-page training and get in front of them over lunch or dinner, and have some one-on-one time. Show them where this goes. Every plus sign is a potential leader.

Some people may just want free oils. They truly have no desire to do a Young Living business. In fact, according to statistics, 92 percent of Young Living distributors are users only. That boggles my mind! Even if your goal isn't to get a generous income, you can get your oils for free with so little effort! One class a month, a 2-hour time commitment a month, would cut it. So if that's their first goal, that's a good place to start. (Though after that first class I'd still put a copy of Gameplan in their hands to help them see the vision of where this goes!)

What does getting your oils for free look like? One class a month, until you have 10 people solidly on Essential Rewards. Ten people under you on ER is enough to get a decent check to pay NingXia for the family or restock your laundry and dish soap. It's very doable.

YOUR ASSIGNMENT: PRACTICE THE TEACHER TRAINING

Your only homework assignment for this chapter is to practice the Teacher Training script and start training your leaders. It's a simple process. Read the 3-page leaders script and give them a tour of the virtual office in person. Make sure you go over the "Rank Qualification" button so they understand what they need to do to rank up. That's it. Then have them do the seven assignments to earn a copy of Gameplan and they are off and running, through one cycle of their Young Living business. And you have a business builder that is lightening your load.

You can teach one class on a Saturday. But if you have 10 leaders doing the same thing, you just taught 11 classes. And that, my friend, is the entire secret to the chessboard of network marketing. Multiply yourself.

CHAPTER 22

HOW TO PRAY OVER YOUR
YOUNG LIVING BUSINESS

This chapter is a bit more hands on. This is probably the most over-looked thing in your entire business. God says that when we come to Him, He is faithful to hear our prayers. He wants abundance for His kids. The trouble is, we never come to Him. And worse yet, when we do, we pray very generic prayers.

I started a habit of praying before each class, publicly, with my team leaders before I taught, from the very first class. I really believe pre-class prayer time with my leaders, plus a prayer journal, as well as collective prayers on our team have been the catapult that exploded our business. Your work means nothing if you do not have favor. You have no favor if you do not ask.

I have a pretty straightforward system for praying, because my memory is atrocious. I went out and bought a little journal. I divided each page into 3 columns: thanks, leaders, goals.

Thanks is just a list of all the amazing things I see God doing. It's something that worked out great. A deal we got on a projector. Unexplained income. A visit from a new, energetic leader. The things I'm grateful for. I like to call them Godwinks.

Leaders are specific prayers for my team. They are the things that are posted and unposted. They are the texts, the stalking I do on their personal pages, the precious nuggets they share from their own lives. I pray diligently and specifically over each of them. I pray for rank. I pray for their families. I pray for OGV. I pray for their burdens. And we lift each other up.

Goals are for my business. I mentioned them earlier: a 100,000 OGV spike. 25,000 a month, 2 legs built to 15,000. I write very specific goals down, then my husband and I pray collectively over them.

One more thing... as you do this—leave a little space to the left of each line. Go through your journal once a week and check off the prayers that were answered. I even like to put a date next to it. It will blow your mind how many prayers God truly answers for us. We just don't pay attention!

YOUR ASSIGNMENT: START A PRAYER JOURNAL

Get a Notebook. Make your columns. Start writing things down. Start praying. BAM. You can practice today by filling in the lines below with 5 Thanks, 5 prayers for your leaders, and 5 business goals.

Also: go rent the movie "The War Room" and watch it. If you are overwhelmed or feel weird about praying, that movie will help tremendously.

Thanks

_____

_____

_____

_____

Leaders

_____

_____

_____

_____

Goals

_____

_____

_____

_____

CHAPTER 23

AVOIDING DISTRACTIONS

Hear my heart on this chapter closely, leader. These things can DESTROY your business. They can take your growth to such a snail's pace that you begin to believe that network marketing doesn't work. It does work. But you have to invest time in areas that make it grow. If you sit around doing make and takes, and statistics show 70% of people never make the product again or order the oils, how does that raise leaders or sell starter kits? You are walking down a dead-end street. Invest in areas that grow. You wouldn't put $1000 in the stock market knowing you'd lose 70%. Why do you spend time in areas that don't grow your business?

Take a few moments and write down the top distractions I see among business builders.

Now be honest. Do you fall into any of these categories? Tell me where you stumble.

Tell me what you can do to change that.

YOUR ASSIGNMENT: FOCUS ON GROWTH

Make a list of what you need to do to grow, and stick to the list. (Hint, hint: hold classes, train leaders, do follow up to get people on Essential Rewards! Write only those 3 things on the lines below.) Every time you are doing a task, ask yourself if it falls under one of those three categories. If it doesn't, why are you wasting your time? If you plateau, open your workbook back to this page and look at the lines below. Hold yourself accountable for how you are spending your time.

Don't fall into the pitfall of wasting time on things that don't grow your business. This truly is simple. Grab the 101 Script and get it in front of as many people as you can, however you are gifted to do that. Train leaders. Contact the people you meet in classes or that get kits. That's it. If you're doing anything outside that, and it's slowing or stopping your ability to teach, your attention is in the wrong place.

CHAPTER 24

ENCOURAGEMENT FOR THE CLIMB

Do you find that you're always looking around you? Looking at other people's rank, wondering why you haven't grown as fast as that girl that signed up the same time you did, wondering why that person signed on that other person's team.

It doesn't matter.

This is a tool that the evil one uses to bait you into giving up. Here's the thing: you write your own story. You craft what you want the outcome to be. If you do it fast, great. If you do it slow, there's nothing wrong with that!

Spend so much time teaching classes and raising leaders that you don't have the time to worry about the muck and the drama around you. Don't look into other's organizations, just look into your own. Be less distracted. Take your business seriously.

Focus on gratitude! What are you grateful for?

YOUR ASSIGNMENT: FOCUS ON WHAT SUCCESS LOOKS LIKE FOR YOU

Take a moment write down what your perfect day would look like. How would you spend your time? What would you do for hobbies? Who would you pour into? Write it down as if it's tomorrow. That's the day you're going for. Don't look at other people's days, focus on yours. And get there. When you are discouraged, come read your perfect day again, envision it in your mind, and go out and schedule a class.

_____

_____

_____

_____

_____

Now I want you to take the Gameplan challenge in this chapter. Sit down and write out your vision. Write down your goals. Make a Gameplan. Open your calendar and schedule a class. Ask three people to invite to it. Don't just say you'll do it or think you'll do it—make it happen. Set a date for your next class TODAY.

The date of that class is: _____

CHAPTER 25

CHEAT SHEET TO GO FROM STARTER KIT TO SILVER

You just finished this whole book. (Make sure you check out the Workbook Appendixes, they are gold too! There is a special Appendix just for you guys!)

Now what do you do? Apply it! If you can't remember want a quick overview of your personal Gameplan, here's a 1-page cheat sheet. As you complete each item, check it off below. Write the date you did it. And hold yourself accountable to the Gameplan book. You control the pace of your way out. It's time to fight for your future.

Order your premium starter kit online (use my number, 1879195, if you have no team.)

Photocopy Appendix A, the Simple 101 Script, from the back of this book and read it.

Make a list of all of your contacts EVERYWHERE. Grab them off Facebook, your Christmas card list, and even former co-workers.

Set up a Facebook event for a class. (Click on "more" then "events" to get to the page). Fill out the description. Use powerful verbs and make the lecture exciting. Put a photo on your event.

Ask 3 people off that list to invite 50 of their friends to the class. They can't just share it to their page, they have go under the "invite friends" button in the event and invite people. Ask them to say something nice about you and the class.

Market the class for 2-3 weeks, no more then 1-2 posts a day.

Open your doors and read that script to the people sitting on your coach. End with a strong close. Tell them where to get the starter kit.

Do good follow up. Call or mail a hand-written note to those that came. (I don't do this by email, it's too impersonal.) Stay in contact. The average person can only say no 7 times.

Rinse and repeat. Teach 4-6 classes a month to aim for Silver in Six. As someone on your team turns to the person next to them and sells their own kit, grab the Teacher Training and train them. Show them "rank qualification" on the Virtual office. Keep in contact with them once a week. Build under two strong leaders to get to silver. When your OGV crosses 10,000 and each leg is over 4,000, you have made it.

Don't hunt people. Don't get lost in the no's. (There will be far more no's then yes's—that's the nature of this business!) Change the philosophy of how you see the business. You are collecting relationships, not starter kits. Don't take it personally when they don't order. Move on, and keep yourself so busy scheduling classes that you don't notice the no's.

Pray. Pray over your business and use Abundance oil abundantly. God has you, and God has this. You were meant to be free. Go out there, world changer. Be bold. Have confidence. And bless all those you meet.

Fill out the Accountability Worksheet in this workbook. (There is also the same form in the Gameplan book). Fill it out every single month to keep you on track. It works!

YOUR ASSIGNMENT: CREATE YOUR PORTABLE OFFICE

Practice putting together your portable office. Grab some small organza bags, a 101 DVD or audio cd, stuff it with flyers and business cards and samples. Carry a few of them with you everywhere and hand them out when you strike up a good conversation. It's a great supplement to classes because it's a portable class. They can listen to an audio cd in their car, and touch base with you afterward.

BONUS TRAINING: HABITS OF A DIAMOND

Put these habits into practice and it will establish trends for you to grow your team.

Practice follow up

Each time someone gets a kit, or expresses interest in a kit, make sure you're sending hand written notes, picking up the phone and calling them, or talking to them in person. Get into the practice of staying in touch with your team.

Raise the level of your own leadership

I don't believe in leadership training that paralyzes you—training where you don't move on your own business. But you've seen a few of my favorite books. I'll add more below. Get them on audio book and spend 15 minutes a day in the car, listening. Grow yourself.

Some of my favs:

- [ ] Gameplan on audio cd—listen to it as you drive every 6 months to regain your focus

- [ ] Gameplan workbook + book set; start a 24 week Gameplan Silver Bootcamp with your own team using these resources. Read a chapter from the book and do a workbook chapter together once a week. If your team is too large to get in a room, do it on Zoom or Facebook Live. (There are bundle discounts for leaders! Check it out at oilabilityteam.com)

- [ ] Robert Kiyosaki Rich Dad, Poor Dad

- [ ] Anything by Jim Rohn

- [ ] Anything by Dani Johnson

- [ ] Anything by Richard Bliss Brook

- [ ] Anything from Eric Worre

- [ ] Monique McClean's Circle of Success

- [ ] Adam Green's 25 to Life: Jailbreak Your 9 to 5

- [ ] Jake Dempsey's Driven for Success: Road Map to the Comp Plan

- [ ] Steve Sheridan's Journey To Health and Wealth

- [ ] The Four Year Career, Young Living Edition

Raise your leaders

Make it a point to connect with your leaders every week. Know how to pray for them. Work with them gently on their weaknesses.

Run your business like a business

Have set business hours. Write them down and stick to them. It works. Even if you can commit only 15 minutes a day, that will make a difference in how you grow.

Schedule your classes at least 2-4 weeks in advance. When I get to the last week of the month, I'll set up Facebook events for the next month's classes. Always stay a month ahead so people know where you are and can commit to coming.

Have fun

Your leaders won't want to do this if they see you working yourself to the bone. I recently flew to Alaska to teach four classes in the Fairbanks area. I took Sunday off to hike with my team, do some whitewater rafting, and soak it all in. There is more to this business then follow up and classes! There are relationships. Don't get so caught up in the sale that you lose best part: those around you.

You have survived the Gameplan Workbook! Congratulations! There are a couple of incredible resources in the Appendix to this book too, so go check them out! And keep an eye out for Gameplan 2, because you'll need it once you hit Silver!

Happy oiling!

Ranking up with Gameplan

I'd like you to practice using some of the tools from the Appendix, because they absolutely work. I already have you practicing the 101 script. One of the things I do is **mail out "business builder boxes."** They are divided into 3 compartments: part one has Gameplan books and workbooks to train 2 to train 2, part two has Fearless books and Fearless calendars pre-printed, and part three has purple bags, that they can be prepared for chance conversations and whenever they are teaching their classes. Part one says "train your leaders." Part two says "follow up." And part three says "teach classes."

I also **hold purple bag stuffing parties** with my team. I use them as contests, because I believe in giving them tools that will help them to grow. The top 5 or 10 people in the contest come to my home where I have purple bags, flyers, all the printables, and everything we need for them to walk out with bags assembled and ready to use. I go through about 100 of them a month myself.

Do a Fearless challenge with your entire team. Have them read the book and accept the 10 challenges, and fill out the calendar. Offer incentives for those not on ER. Offer incentives for those to go up to the next level of ER. It works!

Do Fearless mailings yourself with your zeros, those about to go inactive, on weak legs, or your personally enrolled. Track your results!

Track bootcamp. If you train 2 to train 2 just 12 times, and they duplicate, you'll have an organization of 531,000 and be a Royal Crown Diamond in a year. Does it mean you need to re-watch all the videos? Absolutely not. Just be a coach. Always take 2 new people through bootcamp each month, and be an accountability partner. I like to offer them a Gameplanner for organization and strategy if they take two people through the next month.

Utilize the free tools at oilabilityteam.com. Pray the Moses blessing over your team. Use textable classes- and train your team to use them too. They save time and effort for those that don't show up. Tap into the 70+ free interviews, and use them as training for your leaders. They are inspirational and full of wisdom! There are so many incredible tools right at your fingertips, for free. The Oola page (oilabiltyteam.com/oola) will help your leaders with balance and finding time for their businesses. All their excuses are debunked on one free website.

Thank you for the honor of pouring into you! I look forward to many more years of book writing, and time sharing the things I've learned— and collecting precious nuggets from you that can be shared with team Young Living! We are all DIAMONDS RISING!

-Sarah

Appendix

Oil Ability Gameplan
Accountability and Follow-up

"A dream is just a dream. A goal is a dream with a plan and a deadline." -Harvey MacKay

"A goal without a plan is just a wish." -Anonymous

"Setting goals is the first step in turning the invisible to visible." -Tony Robbins

"People with goals succeed because they know where they are going." -Earl Nightingale

"The plans of the diligent lead to profit as surely as haste leads to poverty." Proverbs 21:5

OIL ABILITY GAMEPLAN ACCOUNTABILITY WORKSHEET

Rules: find a partner, fill it out by the 25th each month, and touch base once a week.

There are only 3 things that grow your business: holding classes, doing follow up, and raising leaders. This chart hones in on those 3 things and helps you set tangible goals and keeps you accountable.

Part 1: Classes

1) Schedule 4-6 classes for the month of: _____

2) Dates of classes scheduled (place a checkmark next to the class if you have set up a Facebook event and asked 3 people to invite 50 different people to it. This should be done before the end of the month so there is time to market classes early in the month.)

Class 1: _____

☐

Class 2: _____

☐

Class 3: _____

☐

Class 4: _____

☐

Class 5: _____

☐

Class 6: _____

☐

3) Overwhelmed by this schedule? A class a week is a commitment of 2 hours a week. That's 8 hours a month. You are giving 160 hours a month to a full time job. This is the job that gets you out of that job. Commit to at least one class a week to grow fast enough that you'll stick with your Young Living business.

Part 2: Business Benchmark Wish List For This Month

OGV growth:_____

Leg growth:

    Leg 1: _____

    Leg 2: _____

This month I am focusing on these legs:_____

This month I am working with these leaders: _____

_____

(write their names and the dates you connected)

    Name: _____

_____

    Dates: _____ , _____ , _____

, _____

    Name: _____

_____

    Dates: _____ , _____ , _____

, _____

    Name: _____

_____

    Dates: _____ , _____ , _____

, _____

Name: _____

_____

Dates: _____ , _____ , _____

, _____

Make sure your leaders get this sheet and also have an accountability partner! Check in with them!

Part 3: Raising Leaders

Write a specific goal on the next sheet for at least two leaders. You should be connecting with your leaders once a week, via phone, text, Facebook, zoom, etc. Tangible goals might be:

- getting the Gameplan book in their hands,
- adding them to your business' Facebook page.
- coming up with a plan to get to convention
- giving them resources like flyers, books, DVD's or CD's
- helping them to teach their first 101 class
- watching them teach a class
- co-teaching a class
- training them to do online classes,
- coaching through their weaknesses
- going through the Teacher Training
- walking them through a Virtual Office tour

- _____
- _____
- _____

Part 4: Follow Up Goals

After each class or Teacher Training, have a plan for following up. For each person that came to class, I make a list of their names and text, call or email them. For each person that got a kit, I mail the package below. For each business builder, I mail the package below. On the back of this sheet, track your mailings.

Sarah's post-class plan (if they get a kit): a Welcome to Young Living book, a Thieves or NingXia flyer, an explanation of Essential Rewards and a list of the Essential Rewards freebies for the month, a DVD or 101 audio CD.

Sarah's post-Teacher Training follow up: the 101 Script in a manilla folder with instructions on how to teach (get 3 people on your couch, read the script, give them your distributor number as sponsor and enroller, rinse and repeat); the Teacher Training in a manilla folder to train them how to raise leaders, the Gameplan book, and links for them to plug in to your team's facebook page and online leadership trainings.

Part 5: Have Set Business Hours

This may not be possible if you have a shift with hours that change, but commit to a certain number of hours worked per week, connecting with leaders, marketing your classes, following up, doing mailings, and teaching classes. Even if you start with 1 hour a week, it's better than no commitment.

Week 1: _____

Week 2: _____

Week 3: _____

Week 4: _____

My best success this month was:

_____

_____

One area I can grow:

_____

_____

My 3-month OGV growth plan:

_____

_____

_____

People that are on my radar (for kits or as leaders):

_____

_____

_____

Congratulations! You made it to the end of the month! Time to start a new accountability sheet!

BOOTCAMP TRACKING

What would happen to your business in one year if you commit to direct income producing activities? What if you committed to teaching one class a week, doing follow up mailings monthly, and training your leaders with bootcamp once a month—for 12 straight months?

You would explode your OGV!

And you would never look back. Make that commitment to bootcamp now. On a calendar (or your Gameplanner) track the day of bootcamp you are on. The system is simple: there are 25 chapters in this book, 25 worksheets in the workbook, and 25 videos at oilabilityteam.com.

EXAMPLE

S	M	T	W	T	F	S
	1	2	3	4	5	6
7	8	9	10	11	12	13
	1	*2*		*3*		
14	15	16	17	18	19	20
		4	*5*			
21	22	23	24	25	26	27
28	29	30	31			

- Pick two people in your organization

- Work with them through the 25 sections—at your own pace (you do not need to re-watch the videos, just be an accountability partner).

- Write the section on the date when you complete it

When they finish, gift them a Gameplanner to keep them focused—but only if they immediately start training two of their own people.

Train two to train two—it works!

Duplication is where you will truly feel the power of Gameplan! Commit to 12 bootcamps and see where it leads!

RINSE + REPEAT.

TRAIN 2 to TRAIN 2

SARAH HARNISCH, GAMEPLAN

FOLLOW UP WITH FEARLESS

Fearless is a powerful tool. When I started using it, my Essential Rewards totals were at 28%. Now, they are tapping 42%. How do I use it effectively? Expect something back.

I called over a thousand zeros on my team and asked why they weren't on ER, and the most common response was that they didn't think of using the oils. They had used the same products for 20, 30, or 40 years—and oils were an afterthought. There is a gap in the education process of training the LIFESTYLE. Fearless isn't a compilation of ways to use the starter kit. It's a tool to train label reading, researching, and practical aromatherapy all rolled into one. If you can train the lifestyle, you'll have a lifelong dedicated oiler. They need to know the why.

Fearless ends with ten challenges to get them oiling every single day and emptying their starter kit. Then it drives hard to Essential Rewards and offers the Simple Swap—a room by room breakdown of the dangers in their home, and what pure Young Living products to use instead.

HOW DO I USE FEARLESS?

After they get their kit, this is the first book I give them. It's an afford-able, duplicatable business tool. I ask them to read Fearless and com-plete the Fearless calendar (available for free at oilabilityteam.com un-der "share" and "Fearless Tools and Resources." They send me a screenshot of their completed calendar. Then I gift them $25 toward their Essential Rewards order once I see it has processed. You can either send a check or call Young Living to place an account credit on their account. Invest back in them and see where it leads. When I offer the

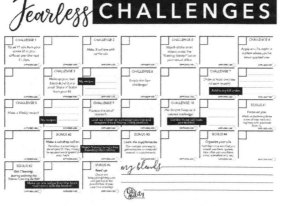

money back, I rarely get a no on completing the challenges. A sin-gle month of ER may yield the return of your $25, depending on the size of their order. And if you build the lifestyle, it's a blessing far greater than that.

IDEAS FOR GETTING PEOPLE ON ESSENTIAL REWARDS

This is a special little nugget that we put together for all of you dedicated workbook users! You can download the full color images online at www.oilabilityteam.com

Tour of Young Living on 50 PV a month with Essential Rewards

Balance and Grow $69.50

Essential Rewards Points Earned 6.95 months 1-3, 13.90 months 4-24, 17.38 months 25+

Tour of Young Living on 50 PV a month with Essential Rewards

Chef Young Living $56.00

Essential Rewards Points Earned 5.60 months 1-3, 11.20 months 4-24, 14.00 months 25+

Tour of Young Living on 50 PV a month with Essential Rewards

Conquer Emotions $51.50

Essential Rewards Points Earned 5.15 months 1-3, 10.30 months 4-24, 12.88 months 25+

Tour of Young Living on 50 PV a month with Essential Rewards

Detox Your Body $59.25

Essential Rewards Points Earned 5.93 months 1-3, 11.85 months 4-24, 14.81 months 25+

Tour of Young Living on 50 PV a month with Essential Rewards

For the Kids $60.75

Essential Rewards Points Earned 6.08 months 1-3, 12.15 months 4-24, 15.19 months 25+

Tour of Young Living on 50 PV a month with Essential Rewards

Frankie Says Relax $54.25

Essential Rewards Points Earned 5.43 months 1-3, 10.85 months 4-24, 13.56 months 25+

Tour of Young Living on 50 PV a month with Essential Rewards

Get Cleaning $50.75

Essential Rewards Points Earned 5.08 months 1-3, 10.15 months 4-24, 12.69 months 25+

Tour of Young Living on 50 PV a month with Essential Rewards

Intro to Supplements $57.50

Essential Rewards Points Earned 5.75 months 1-3, 11.50 months 4-24, 14.38 months 25+

Tour of Young Living on 50 PV a month with Essential Rewards

Old MacDonald Had a Farm $64.50

Essential Rewards Points Earned 5.70 months 1-3, 11.40 months 4-24, 14.25 months 25+

Tour of Young Living on 50 PV a month with Essential Rewards

Oral Care $50.00

Essential Rewards Points Earned 5.00 months 1-3, 10.00 months 4-24, 12.50 months 25+

Tour of Young Living on 50 PV a month with Essential Rewards

Personal Care $50.50

Essential Rewards Points Earned 5.05 months 1-3, 10.10 months 4-24, 12.63 months 25+

Tour of Young Living on 50 PV a month with Essential Rewards

Rock Your Body $52.00

Essential Rewards Points Earned 5.20 months 1-3, 10.40 months 4-24, 13.00 months 25+

Tour of Young Living on 190 PV a month with Essential Rewards

The Complete Bathroom Kit= $192.25

Essential Rewards Points Earned 19.23 months 1-3, 38.45 months 4-24, 48.06 months 25+
Plus all the free oils on the 190PV Level of Essential Rewards Freebies.

Tour of Young Living on 190 PV a month with Essential Rewards

Chemical Free Kids=$205.25

Essential Rewards Points Earned 20.53 months 1-3, 41.05 months 4-24, 51.31 months 25+
Plus all the free oils on the 190PV Level of Essential Rewards Freebies.

Tour of Young Living on 190 PV a month with Essential Rewards

Energy=$201.75

Essential Rewards Points Earned 20.18 months 1-3, 40.35 months 4-24, 50.44 months 25+
Plus all the free oils on the 190PV Level of Essential Rewards Freebies.

Tour of Young Living on 190 PV a month with Essential Rewards

For Little Noses=$240.25

Essential Rewards Points Earned 19.45 months 1-3, 38.90 months 4-24, 48.63 months 25+
Plus all the free oils on the 190PV Level of Essential Rewards Freebies.

Tour of Young Living on 190 PV a month with Essential Rewards

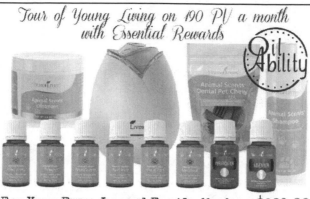

For Your Four-Legged Family Member=$269.00

Essential Rewards Points Earned 19.75 months 1-3, 39.50 months 4-24, 49.38 months 25+
Plus all the free oils on the 190PV Level of Essential Rewards Freebies.

Tour of Young Living on 190 PV a month with Essential Rewards

Just Breathe=$276.50

Essential Rewards Points Earned 19.20 months 1-3, 38.40 months 4-24, 48.00 months 25+
Plus all the free oils on the 190PV Level of Essential Rewards Freebies.

Tour of Young Living on 190 PV a month with Essential Rewards

Mini Beauty School=$200.75

Essential Rewards Points Earned 20.08 months 1-3, 40.15 months 4-24, 50.19 months 25+
Plus all the free oils on the 190PV Level of Essential Rewards Freebies.

Tour of Young Living on 190 PV a month with Essential Rewards

Muscles & Bones=$195.50

Essential Rewards Points Earned 19.55 months 1-3, 39.10 months 4-24, 48.88 months 25+
Plus all the free oils on the 190PV Level of Essential Rewards Freebies.

Tour of Young Living on 190 PV a month with Essential Rewards

Oils in the Bedroom = $225.75

Essential Rewards Points Earned 22.58 months 1-3, 45.15 months 4-24, 56.44 months 25+
Plus all the free oils on the 190PV Level of Essential Rewards Freebies.

Tour of Young Living on 190 PV a month with Essential Rewards

Prayer Time=$215.75

Essential Rewards Points Earned 19.20 months 1-3, 38.40 months 4-24, 48.00 months 25+
Plus all the free oils on the 190PV Level of Essential Rewards Freebies.

Tour of Young Living on 190 PV a month with Essential Rewards

Relax=$215.75

Essential Rewards Points Earned 21.58 months 1-3, 43.15 months 4-24, 53.94 months 25+
Plus all the free oils on the 190PV Level of Essential Rewards Freebies.

Tour of Young Living on 190 PV a month with Essential Rewards

Comes with: Melrose, Raven, RC,
DiGize Vitality, EndoFlex Vitality,
Thieves Vitality, and JuvaFlex Vitality

Support Your Immune System=$202.50

Essential Rewards Points Earned 20.25 months 1-3, 40.50 months 4-24, 50.63 months 25+
Plus all the free oils on the 190PV Level of Essential Rewards Freebies.

Tour of Young Living on 300 PV a month with Essential Rewards

Supplements= $321.25

Essential Rewards Points Earned 30.83 months 1-3, 61.65 months 4-24, 77.06 months 25+
Plus all the free oils on the 300PV Level of Essential Rewards Freebies

Tour of Young Living on 300 PV a month with Essential Rewards

Beauty=$309.00

Essential Rewards Points Earned 30.90 months 1-3, 61.80 months 4-24, 77.25 months 25+
Plus all the free oils on the 300PV Level of Essential Rewards Freebies

Tour of Young Living on 300 PV a month with Essential Rewards

Build that Business= $306.75

Essential Rewards Points Earned 30.68 months 1-3, 61.35 months 4-24, 76.69 months 25+
Plus all the free oils on the 300PV Level of Essential Rewards Freebies

Tour of Young Living on 300 PV a month with Essential Rewards

Chef Young Living= $332.75

Essential Rewards Points Earned 30.73 months 1-3, 61.46 months 4-24, 76.84 months 25+
Plus all the free oils on the 300PV Level of Essential Rewards Freebies

Tour of Young Living on 300 PV a month with Essential Rewards

Chef Young Living= $332.75
Essential Rewards Points Earned 30.73
Plus all the free oils on the 300PV Level of Essential Rewards Freebies

Tour of Young Living on 300 PV a month with Essential Rewards

Cleanse those Toxins= $309.75
Essential Rewards Points Earned 30.98 months 1-3, 61.95 months 4-24, 77.44 months 25+
Plus all the free oils on the 300PV Level of Essential Rewards Freebies

Tour of Young Living on 300 PV a month with Essential Rewards

Comes with:
Harmony, Forgiveness, Inner Child,
Present Time, Release, and Valor II

Feel All the Emotions= $312.00
Essential Rewards Points Earned 31.20 months 1-3, 62.40 months 4-24, 78.00 months 25+
Plus all the free oils on the 300PV Level of Essential Rewards Freebies

Tour of Young Living on 300 PV a month with Essential Rewards

Focus on All the Things= $309.25

Essential Rewards Points Earned 30.93 months 1-3, 61.85 months 4-24, 77.31 months 25+
Plus all the free oils on the 300PV Level of Essential Rewards Freebies

Tour of Young Living on 300 PV a month with Essential Rewards

Comes with:
Tummygize, SniffleEase, Sleepyize,
Owie, GeneYus, and BiteBuster

For the Little Ones= $306.75

Essential Rewards Points Earned 30.68 months 1-3, 61.35 months 4-24, 76.69 months 25+
Plus all the free oils on the 300PV Level of Essential Rewards Freebies

Tour of Young Living on 300 PV a month with Essential Rewards

Get Cleaning= $301.00

Essential Rewards Points Earned 30.10 months 1-3, 60.20 months 4-24, 75.25 months 25+
Plus all the free oils on the 300PV Level of Essential Rewards Freebies

Tour of Young Living on 300 PV a month with Essential Rewards

Get Rolling and Moving= $316.50

Essential Rewards Points Earned 31.65 months 1-3, 63.30 months 4-24, 79.13 months 25+
Plus all the free oils on the 300PV Level of Essential Rewards Freebies

Tour of Young Living on 300 PV a month with Essential Rewards

 +

Comes with:
Aloes, Cassia, Cedarwood, Cypress,
Frankincense, Hyssop, Myrrh, Myrtle,
Onycha, and Rose of Sharon.

Oils of Ancient Scripture= $311.00

Essential Rewards Points Earned 31.10 months 1-3, 62.20 months 4-24, 77.75 months 25+
Plus all the free oils on the 300PV Level of Essential Rewards Freebies

Tour of Young Living on 300 PV a month with Essential Rewards

Rock Your Body= $306.75

Essential Rewards Points Earned 30.40 months 1-3, 60.80 months 4-24, 76.00 months 25+
Plus all the free oils on the 300PV Level of Essential Rewards Freebies

OIL ABILITY RESOURCES TO CATAPULT YOUR TEAM

Since Gameplan was first released, the Oil Ability team has been on the forefront of ground-breaking sharing tools that make getting to Diamond even easier. For me, the goal is to make your path to Diamond shorter than mine was. Thousands of people have used these tools with terrific success.

When I saw the business opportunity (I mean TRULY saw it) — and I knew where this went, I wanted it for everyone, no matter what their gift set was. Not everyone can comfortably stand in front of a room of 20 people Not everyone can read well. Public speaking is not everyone's way of sharing. An online format isn't necessarily everyone's way of sharing, either.

But I believe anyone can be free. So I started to develop tools that made it simpler to share. That's what this entire section is about. If you are afraid, this will take the fear out of the passion you have for oils. Let's work together to get oils into every home in the world.

BOOKS

Gameplan: A Comprehensive Strategy Guide to go from Starter Kit to Silver. This is the book that started it all; over 1.5 million copies sold in a year. Thousands have used Gameplan to explode their OGV and hit rank after rank. Once you finish reading it, pick two leaders and train two to train two. Have them read the 25 chapters in the book, do the 25 worksheets in the workbook, and watch the 25 free Bootcamp videos for the full system. The Gameplan you hold in your hands has been revised with over 50 pages of new content, and updated information for the Starter kit.

Gameplan Workbook: This is a companion workbook that makes the book come alive for your team. It puts action to your dreams and goals. This isn't just a fill-in-the-blank workbook. It helps you put action to your goals chapter by chapter. This is the accountability tool to help you train your team to duplicate!

Your Gameplan: This mini book is the first prospecting book in all of Young Living, designed to be affordable to share and to effectively draw members to your team. This explains Sarah's story from rags to riches, shows the Income Disclosure Guide, gives eight reasons for doing a

Young Living business, and poses the questions, "Will their 40 hour a week job get them out of where they are? Can they cross things off their bucket list?" If the answer is no, it's time to re-evaluate. This is the book that gets them stacking up a Young Living business against how they are spending their time right now, then coming back to you to get trained.

Fearless, Confidence with Essential Oils in 2 Hours: This is the top oils training guide in all of Young Living. Why? It gently trains new oilers to research, label read, look critically at things in their home, accept 10 oiling challenges and oil with purpose and deliberation every day. It's an affordable training system for aromatherapy, the perfect place to start when someone gets their kit. It will take the fear out of using their oils, and educates them onto essential rewards. Pass these mini books out like candy with the free Fearless calendar at oilabilityteam.com. Sarah uses these in purple bags, in every class she teaches, in follow up mailings and care packages, and to members who are about to go inactive.

Gameplanner: This planner was put together after over a year of research and study of hundreds of other planning systems. It's the first revolving planner designed for network marketing. Every three months, it's pulled down off the website and new months are added, so if you have a leader explode in June, they can still get a full year of accountability. This is the glue that makes the entire Gameplan system stick for your budding leaders. It keeps them laser focused on teaching classes, getting people on Essential Rewards, and training their leaders. Each edition of the Gameplanner includes:

- rank mapping pages to strategically plan the path to the next rank
- stat tracking pages to catch your weaknesses before you feel them in your OGV
- Gameplan bootcamp tracking sheets to train your team
- Sheets to track mileage, and essential rewards orders for tax purposes
- A list of all the important dates in Young Living for the upcoming year
- Space for a vision board and debt pay-off goals
- warm and cold market lists
- daily business goals and schedule outline
- Space for planning weekly training and tracking contests

- prayer journal pages
- a full list of every oil Young Living has to help track as you build your collection

Plus beautiful full color photos of the farms and over 250 inspirational Gameplan quotes.

This planner is AWESOME. And it gets results. Sarah gifts these to every person on her team that trains two people with Bootcamp.

DVD'S

Intro to Young Living 2 DVD set: *Essential Oils 101* and *Why Do Young Living As A Business.* The 101 DVD is the first video; a ground up lecture where it all started; centers on the Premium Starter Kit. Sarah generated this for leaders that were too timid to teach. Just pop the DVD in, play hostess, and pass around the Starter Kit. It includes the bold close on the end. Why Do Young Living As A Business is what helped grow 800 Oil Ability leaders in 18 months. It's the Your Gameplan mini in DVD form. Sarah shows this 12-minute video after every class she teaches to pick up business builders. *50 minutes total*

Gameplan Live: This is the 35-hour Gameplan bootcamp in two hours. It's what Sarah teaches when she is on tour!. She uses it as a kick off when she does new bootcamps with her team, as a refresher to those that have been through bootcamp, or as a resource at team retreats. *2 hours*

The Complete Gameplan DVD Training System: This set contains over five hours of training; including a 60-minute compliance DVD (the only compliance training in all of Young Living), a new lecture called Oily Lifestyle, the full 101 class, a full Teacher Training DVD for you to use to train you leaders that are long distance, Why Do Young Living As A Business (the mini on DVD), and How To Fill Classes Without Knowing People. Also includes the Scavenger Hunt video, a four minute icebreaker video for your classes, featuring Sarah's five kids showing off what an oil-infused house looks like. This can be used in 101 classes to break up your lecture and introduce your audience to a personal tour of a chemical-free home. This video has gotten rave reviews and is a tremendous asset to your teaching!! *5 hours*

CD/AUDIOS

Essential Oils 101: This is an extremely powerful tool for busy potential oilers to listen to in the car. It's been called the best tool, save Gameplan, that the team has put together. Pass them out in purple bags. *45 minutes.*

Toxin Free Life: This is an entire class on the Thieves Starter kit that will rock your world. Use for people that are not ready yet for oils, to introduce them to a clean living lifestyle, or for those that have already been to a 101 class and are looking for more knowledge on different Young Living products. These can also be used in purple bags. 30 minutes

Gameplan: The Gameplan book is available in audio format via iTunes or Audible!!! Professionally recorded and read by the author. This is an amazing tool for those that have finished reading the Gameplan book. She gifts it to leaders as they finish bootcamp, to continue training their brain. You can listen on a cell phone, tablet, or computer. Find it on oilabilityteam.com or Amazon. *Over 5 hours*

Fearless, Confidence with Essential Oils in 2 Hours: Fearless hit number one on Amazon for Aromatherapy, and has remained in the top five for half a year. It's the top oils training guide in all of Young Living. Why? It gently trains people to research, label read, look critically at things in their home, accept ten oiling challenges and oil with purpose and deliberation every day. It's now available on iTunes or Audible. Read by the author and recorded in a professional studio. Let her radio voice lull you to absorb and apply aromatherapy knowledge! *2 hours*

FREE ON OILABILITYTEAM.COM

- "Textable" classes
- Free Essential Rewards marketing images
- Dozens of interviews with corporate employees at the farms and Young Living Diamonds
- One of the most powerful videos recorded on the business: "Sarah's Why" video, to fire up your team
- 101 and Toxin Free Life audio classes, to download and burn onto CD yourself!
- A full beauty school class
- Powerpoint slides to go with the 101 script in this book

- The Moses blessing
- Links to all the ingredients for the Famous Purple Bags.
- Updates on Sarah's speaking schedule and Gameplan Live events

You can connect with Sarah on Facebook. Oil Ability with Sarah Is a great place to send your leaders and team members for business education. Every Tuesday night, Sarah does a live Gameplan Roundtable at 8:30 p.m. eastern where you can ask your business questions and win prizes!

Made in the USA
Middletown, DE
31 October 2018